COGNITIVE DIVERSITY
AT WORK™
Third Edition

COGNITIVE DIVERSITY AT WORK™
Third Edition

Helping people who think differently to work together

The sky is filled with stars, invisible by day
Henry Wadsworth Longfellow

Great minds can think differently
Anon

Michael Davis

ISBN 979-8-3290-3560-5
Published by Cognitive Diversity Ltd 2024.
Font: Bembo 12pt
This paperback edition matches the Kindle eBook Cognitive Diversity At Work™ Third Edition published 2024.

Cover illustration by Cognitive Diversity Ltd
Credit: Cover photo by Greg Rakozy on Unsplash
Illustrations by Cognitive Diversity Ltd

Disclaimer
This book contains information about cognitive diversity. The information is not advice and should not be treated as advice. If you need professional advice, please consult Michael Davis: md@cognitivediversity.co.uk.

I dedicate this book to my wife Jennifer,
whose relational thinking shows me the way.

Michael Davis

Introduction

Many years ago, I was asked by a psychologist: "Why is project management so left brained?" Although I was a project manager, I could not answer the question. It set me off on a journey of discovery to find an answer. After many years of new learning, research, and training I can now easily answer the question. In fact, I can now easily answer far bigger questions such as: how can you help people who think differently to work together?

At work, do you have misunderstandings, mistakes, false understandings, confrontation, or tribal groupthink with other people but don't know why? Do you work well with some people and not others, but don't know why? The reasons are invisible but can be revealed through the powerful insights of cognitive diversity. It's startling, like realising that the stars also shine in the daytime. The insights are available to anyone, in any job, anywhere.

The old binary model of left and right brain thinking is too simplistic. The new model of cognitive diversity comprises four quadrants: *upper left, lower left, lower right,* and *upper right.* In each quadrant we can measure the strength of thinking on a scale from 0 to 100. We can therefore produce a highly detailed cognitive diversity profile for any individual, pair, team, and organisation at work.

We can also produce a highly detailed cognitive diversity profile for any job. For example, the 59 topics describing project management can be plotted over all four quadrants, and not simply lumped together in one half of the brain (1). Thinking is the basis of everything you do at work. Thinking precedes what you do, why you do it, how you do it, and how you relate to other people.

If you want powerful insights into areas such as: stereotyping in education; the blindness of groupthink; the key to job satisfaction; getting more emotional intelligence into boardrooms; the difference between male and female entrepreneurs; the damaging effects of bureaucracy; challenges facing lawyers, doctors, and teachers at work; the UK's damaging handling of COVID-19, and why there are fewer women than men in STEM careers, then this is the book for you.

If you want higher performance through improving your communicating, collaborating, decision-making, problem-solving, coaching, mentoring, counselling and customer relations, then this is the book for you.

If you want higher productivity and staff retention, more creativity and innovation, and quicker job-mastery, then this is the book for you.

If you want to know how cognitive diversity is above the identity diversity of Diversity, Equity and Inclusion, then this is the book for you.

This practical business book gives worked examples of cognitive diversity in the workplace by using real-world case studies. These case studies form the basis of a body of knowledge which can be used for teaching and research. In Fair Use terms the sources of the case studies are factual accounts in the media, after the fact, and cannot affect the market for the original work. Only people who are deemed to have placed themselves in the public domain are named. No infringement of copyright is intended. References are indicated by ( ). The views expressed in this book are those of the author alone.

Contents

Introduction vii

Chapter 1. Cognitive Diversity.................................. 1

Why cognitive diversity? 1

What is cognitive diversity?.................................. 2

What is Cognitive Diversity At Work™?................. 3

What is Cognitive Diversity At Work™ not?........... 5

Cognitive diversity is above identity diversity 9

Chapter 2. Cognitive Diversity Profiling.................. 11

What is profiling based on? 11

How is an Individual Profile created? 12

The profiling method is well-proven 15

The profiling method is unique............................ 15

Cognitive Diversity At Work™ illustrated 16

Individual Profile dominant thinking.................... 16

Get your own Individual Profile 18

Profiling, consultancy, and workshops 19

Chapter 3. Can Your Individual Profile Change? 21

Chapter 4: End Stereotyping at Work.................... 25

Men and women thinking at work........................ 25

End the myth of stereotyping.............................. 26

Chapter 5: End Groupthink at Work.................... 29

The meaning of your communication 29

Communication at work...................................... 29

The most difficult communication 29

Difficult communication..................................... 30

Less difficult communication............................... 31

Easier communication................................. 31

The easiest communication: groupthink 32

End the blindness of groupthink at work 34

Chapter 6: Male and Female Brains........................ 35

'Brains are a mixed bag' 35

'Men and women see things differently'............... 37

Chapter 7: Empathy, Sympathy, and Productivity 39

Empathy and sympathy at work....................... 39

Productivity at work................................ 41

Chapter 8: Job Satisfaction............................ 43

Maximising job satisfaction.......................... 43

What's important to young job seekers 43

Top five jobs desired................................ 44

Top five jobs actually performed 46

Check your job satisfaction 46

Chapter 9: Social Mobility............................. 49

The privilege gap and social mobility.................. 49

How can cognitive diversity help social mobility? .. 50

Chapter 10: Directors, and Entrepreneurs................ 53

Emotional intelligence in the boardroom.............. 53

Are entrepreneurs male only? 54

Chapter 11: Men and Relational Thinking.............. 59

Some men can struggle to talk........................ 59

'Men tend to be solitary' 60

Male reporters called 'emotional retards' 61

Chapter 12: Letting Agents Anger Tenants.............. 63

An example of most difficult communication......... 63

'We should have been more empathetic.' 65

Chapter 13: Cognitive Diversity in the Law 67

Trial left a family 'a smoking wreck' 67

'Sheltering behind legalese is a cop-out' 69

Grenfell Tower fire: judge accused of 'disrespect' 70

Chapter 14: Cognitive Diversity in Health 73

Growing a bedside manner 73

Harmful arrogance in the operating theatre 74

'Ten-minute appointments are unfit for purpose' 76

District nurses becoming 'task-focused' 77

Why do some women quit surgical training? 78

Why do some trained female surgeons quit? 80

A surgeon's tale: analyse first, reflect later 82

Chapter 15: Cognitive Diversity in Education 85

Potential shortage of teachers in England 85

Teaching is a vocation 86

Newly qualified teachers drop out 86

Experienced teachers drop out 87

Three main reasons for leaving teaching 88

Anecdotal evidence of bureaucracy 89

Bureaucracy versus teaching...................91

Chapter 16: Women in STEM 93

'Girls don't like physics' 93

The STEM pipeline 94

So, what is STEM? 95

How many girls take STEM A levels? 98

Gender stereotypes in STEM A levels? 102

Gender stereotypes in any A levels? 103

How many women work in STEM? 106

Do we need more women in STEM? 108

Can teachers inspire more girls into STEM? 108

Can teachers inspire girls into STEM trades? 112

Can anyone else inspire girls into STEM? 112

Are women choosing to work outside STEM? 113

Chapter 17: The UK's Handling of COVID-19 119

Finding insights 119

No UK strategic plan for a coronavirus pandemic 120

The UK's border controls 121

SAGE advice to the UK Government.................. 123

The role of 'nudging' in stoking fears 124

'Everyone is at risk'............................. 125

Everyone was not at the same level of risk 128

The first wave and lockdown 1 130

Hospitals close to breaking point 132

The second wave and lockdowns 2 and 3 133

The social damage of lockdowns 135

The health damage of lockdowns 137

The education damage of lockdowns................. 141

The economic damage of lockdowns................. 142

'Focused Protection not lockdown' 146

'Lockdown policies should be rejected'.............. 149

'Groupthink silenced opponents of lockdowns' 150

Social media companies helped anti-vaxxers......... 153

'UK should make better use of data' 154

The Delta wave of mid 2021 155

The Omicron wave of late 2021 157

The BMJ recommendations................................157

SAGE stands down...161

The UK's COVID-19 cognitive diversity profile ..162

Recommendations 163

Conclusion and Next Steps 167

Acknowledgements...169

References..171

About the Author 175

Chapter 1. Cognitive Diversity

Why cognitive diversity?

There is growing recognition of the benefits of cognitive diversity in the workplace.

In 2018 Mark Carney, then Governor of the Bank of England, wrote to the Rt Hon Nicky Morgan MP, then Chair of the Parliamentary Treasury Committee, stating that: 'The Bank defines diversity as both 'who we are' *(identity diversity)* and 'how we think' *(cognitive diversity)* (my italics).

Admiral Sir Tony Radakin, appointed UK Chief of the Defence Staff in November 2021, said that under his stewardship every aspect of leadership in Britain's Armed Forces would be done better, and warned that if the diversity of the UK was not reflected in the services, "...we risk looking ridiculous...this is not about wokefulness. It is about woefulness. The woefulness...of not reflecting the ethnic, religious, and cognitive diversity of our nation".

Professor Margaret Heffernan, a mentor to CEOs and senior executives of major global organizations, has written that '...cognitive diversity is...an insurance policy against internally generated blindness that leaves institutions exposed and out of touch'. This book shows that the blindness is due to employing people who think alike and who develop groupthink. Cognitive diversity matters at work because it shows how to guard against groupthink.

Brian Langston QPM, a retired police Assistant Chief Constable, wrote that '...the quest for identity diversity in the police service was misguided and unachievable, and should be replaced with cognitive diversity'.

Terry Ellis of GE Partners has written 'cognitive diversity...can broaden the appeal of future products...and drive different ways of thinking, and often profit'.

Frank Luntz, referred to as 'the world's most influential political pundit', has said: "No diversity is more important than diversity of thought."

What is cognitive diversity?

Ned Herrmann (2) showed that all adults worldwide at work - regardless of gender, ethnicity and culture - have access to the same four types of thinking: analytical, practical, relational, and experimental. Herrmann called this Whole Brain® Thinking, which we use as our model for cognitive diversity.

In Whole Brain® Thinking your cognitive diversity lies in your personal strength of preference for each way of thinking. Your strengths can be measured and summarised as strong, intermediate, or low. A quick metaphor for visualising the three strengths is:

analytical	experimental
analytical	experimental
analytical	experimental
practical	relational
practical	relational
practical	relational

Four ways of thinking at work, three strengths

A quick metaphor for visualising my cognitive diversity is:

analytical	experimental
practical	relational

The thinking preferences of Michael Davis

Hence, you have your own individual cognitive diversity. When you work with another individual, your combined cognitive diversity as a pair can be measured. When you work with other individuals in a team, your combined cognitive diversity as a team can be measured. Even the cognitive diversity of your organisation can be measured.

What is Cognitive Diversity At Work™?

Cognitive Diversity At Work™ is the application of Whole Brain® Thinking cognitive diversity in any type of work.

It shows a very strong correlation between your thinking preferences and your related interests, skills, competences, and the type of work that gives you most job satisfaction.

It is fact-based, brain-based, and thinking-based. It is fully internalised, it is your way of preferred thinking, moulded by your individual nature and nurture.

It is purely positive. It does not measure negative thinking. For example, if you hate mathematics, it will show that you have a very low to zero preference for mathematics. In nature, there is no such thing as a negative. 'Negative' is a human mental construct.

It is measurable and your Individual Profile can be created.

It is totally reliable for cross-organisational comparisons; all profiles are produced to the same standard, and the profiling method is neutral and unbiased.

It addresses root causes since thinking determines behaviour. For example, in project management the major cause of project failure is often cited as 'poor communication'. Poor communication is in fact a symptom of underlying root causes which need to be addressed, so that the outcome is good communication. Knowing how you prefer to think, and how others prefer to think, is a great start in creating rapport as the basis for better communication. Cognitive Diversity At Work™ sees you firstly as a 'thinker' and secondly as a 'doer' at work.

It is scalable and works at four levels: the individual, the pair, the team, and the organisation:

Credits. Adam Winger, Team SEO, Alex Kotliarskyi. All on Unsplash

Cognitive diversity works at all four levels

It fully satisfies the definition of inclusion set by Abbott Laboratories (3). It builds a foundation whereby you can reach your full potential by:

- making you aware of your own thinking preferences, and making you aware that other people can have different thinking preferences

- inviting you to recognise and accept the different thinking preferences of other people

- inviting you to respect the different thinking preferences of other people

4

- enabling you to understand where others are coming from and enabling you to think situationally and adjust your behaviour for the best outcomes.

What is Cognitive Diversity At Work™ not?

It is not related to identity diversity, which is the 'D' in Diversity, Equity and Inclusion. It does not use the language of identity diversity. In the UK, the government monitors its workforce in terms of identity diversity (also known as demographic diversity), which is defined in terms of biological sex, gender identity, ethnicity, sexual orientation, disability, religious faith or belief, age, and class. The government does not − at the time of writing - monitor its workforce in terms of how people think. Identity diversity is about 'what you are' or 'how you identify yourself' and does not include 'how you think at work'.

Research by the McKinsey consultancy has been widely used by business groups and campaigners to push for changes in the way employers recruit staff and apprentices. McKinsey claimed that ethnicity diversity '…is a business imperative that drives real business results'. However, a major new study by Jeremiah Green, professor of accounting at Texas A&M University, and John Hand, professor of accounting at the University of North Carolina at Chapel Hill, could not reproduce the McKinsey findings. Their study in *Econ Journal Watch* says that there is no evidence that ethnically diverse management teams boost profits.

It is not multi-tasking in the sense of thinking analytically, practically, relationally, and experimentally all at the same time. It is better to think in each way in turn when problem-solving or decision-making, in a Whole Brain® Walk Around. Psychologist Audrey Tang said, "What we like to call multi-tasking is not − it's attention-splitting…doing two (or more) cognitive things at once results in a lower quality of output".

It is internalised and not externalised. Your thinking preferences are not externally imposed in the way that identity diversity polices can be imposed on you by an organisation.

It is not political. As Professor Margaret Heffernan has written: 'Cognitive diversity is not a form of political correctness'.

It is not context specific. It is independent of context. There is no need to look for a context.

It is not 'neurodiversity'. For example, both GCHQ and BAE Systems have stated that they wish to attract more neurodiverse women to work for them in cybersecurity jobs. They define neurodiversity in terms of autism spectrum disorder, dyslexia, attention deficit hyperactivity disorder (ADHD), dyscalculia, and dyspraxia. They find that 'neurodiversity' brings benefits to roles that require faster and better pattern recognition, sharper accuracy, and greater attention to detail.

It is not neuroscience, which is the study of the entire nervous system not just the brain.

It is not negative. It is purely positive.

It is not Neuro-Linguistic Programming (NLP), which is how the brain can be reprogrammed linguistically. NLP teaches that the brain (neuro) is programmed when experiencing life through the five senses: sight, hearing (linguistic), physical feeling and touch, smell, and taste.

It is not the same as other forms of thinking, such as your set of values or beliefs. Your values are what are important to you. For example, your values may include family, faith, security, reputation, free speech, power, money, health, job title, prestige, friendships, fame, sports team, number of likes on social media, work-life balance, and so on. Your beliefs are what you believe to be true, without any evidence for doing so.

It is not your *state of mind* such as being sad, happy, angry, confident, anxious, worried, determined, relaxed or calm. An intense state of mind can actually prevent you from thinking rationally – as I discovered to my horror when I accidentally deleted this book from my hard drive, and when the web-hosting service lost the companion website during a server upgrade.

It is not the same as IQ (Intelligence Quotient). Your IQ number is a measure of your analytical dexterity with numerical and linguistic reasoning. Examples include the 11 plus examination for UK grammar school, or the worldwide Graduate Management Admissions Test (GMAT) for MBA business school.

As such, IQ represents only a fraction of your possible intelligence. According to Harvard professor Howard Gardner, human beings have at least seven distinct forms of intelligence (4). He defined intelligence as the ability to solve problems or fashion products that are valued in at least one cultural setting or community. Professor Gardner's list of seven intelligences included:-

- logical (numeracy) *(analytical thinking)*

- linguistic (literacy) *(analytical thinking)*

- spatial: appreciation of large spaces and/or local spatial layouts such as architecture, art, sculpture *(experimental thinking)*

- musical: capacity to create and perceive musical patterns such as composing, orchestrating, playing, conducting *(analytical, practical, relational thinking)*

- bodily kinaesthetic: ability to solve problems or create products using the whole body or parts of the body such as manual work, dancing, sports, gymnastics, singing, acting *(practical, relational thinking)*

- interpersonal emotional: the understanding of other people such as coaching, mentoring, counselling, psychiatry *(relational thinking)*

- intrapersonal emotional: the understanding of oneself *(relational thinking)*.

Beyond careers based on numeracy and literacy, people can and do enjoy rewarding and successful careers as landscapers, gardeners, architects, artists, sculptors, photographers, musicians, conductors, singers, actors, dancers, footballers, cricketers, golfers, tennis players, jockeys, coaches, counsellors, and clergy, for example. And how such people enrich life for the rest of us! Fortunate is the student whose school nurtures all seven intelligences.

It seems that state schooling cannot afford to nurture all seven intelligences. Take art for example. The journalist Andrew Marr, a keen painter, was reported to be '...really upset that the UK is being robbed of the next David Hockney...we have now several generations of kids coming through schools who have never been taught the basics of drawing.'

It is not the same as your style, skills, or competencies. You may have been forced by circumstances beyond your control into a job that you dislike or even hate. Yet you have developed sufficient skills and competences to get by, get paid, put food on the table, and keep a roof over your head. It is not simply a box-ticking formality for consuming Learning and Development budget. It is a serious, practical business tool.

It is not some management fad, doomed to disappear. It's been bringing benefits since the 1980s.

Cognitive diversity is above identity diversity

Ned Herrmann showed that all adults worldwide at work regardless of gender, ethnicity and culture have access to Whole Brain® Thinking cognitive diversity. This can be visualised as:

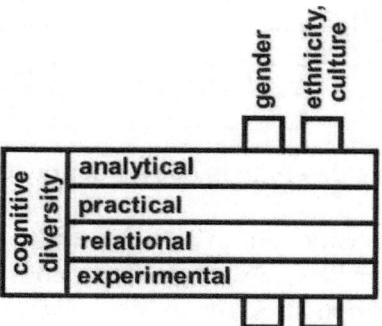

Whole Brain® Thinking cognitive diversity is accessed by all genders, ethnicities and cultures

If we add to gender, ethnicity and culture we arrive at the definition of identity diversity:

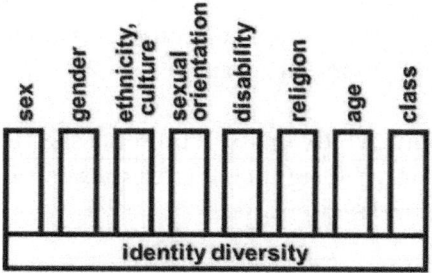

This leads us to a relationship between cognitive diversity and identity diversity. To illustrate how cognitive diversity is above identity diversity, we use the graphic overleaf which is a registered design of Cognitive Diversity Ltd:

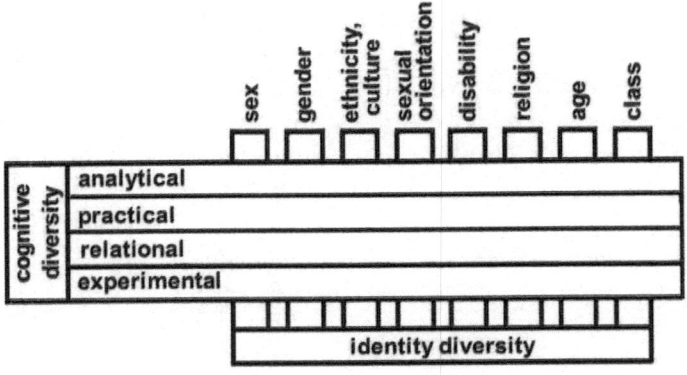

Cognitive diversity is above identity diversity

Cognitive Diversity At Work™ states that all adults worldwide, regardless of sex, gender identity, ethnicity and culture, sexual orientation, disability, religious faith or belief, age, and class have access to the four types of thinking: analytical, practical, relational, and experimental.

When you think of someone at work in terms of their cognitive diversity, you automatically cover any possible combination of their identity diversity. Conversely, when you think of someone at work only in terms of identity diversity, you ignore their cognitive diversity: you don't know how they prefer to think.

Note how cognitive diversity represents the thinking within a single brain, and the eight characteristics of identity diversity are separate, unrelated entities.

Chapter 2. Cognitive Diversity Profiling

What is profiling based on?

Profiling is based on the Whole Brain® Model (5):

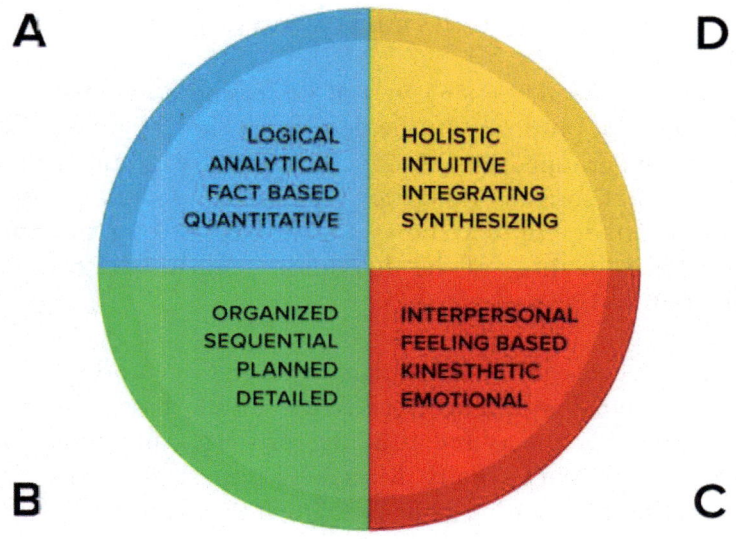

The Whole Brain® Model

The four-colour, four-quadrant graphic, and Whole Brain® are registered trademarks of Herrmann Global LLC. With kind permission of Herrmann®.

It is a metaphorical model that is linked to the physical structures of the brain and is fact-based and brain-based. Instead of the two halves of the simple left-brain/right-brain model, there are four quadrants of thinking summarised by four descriptors of thinking:-

- *upper left* A quadrant: analytical thinking - logical, analytical, fact-based, quantitative: typical jobs include lawyer, engineer, doctor, financier

- *lower left* B quadrant: practical thinking - organised, sequential, planned, detailed: typical jobs are in accountancy, insurance, the civil service, quality assurance, operations, project management

- *lower right* C quadrant: relational thinking – interpersonal, feeling based, kinesthetic, emotional: typical jobs include teacher, trainer, nurse, sales

- *upper right* D quadrant: experimental thinking – holistic, intuitive, integrating, synthesising; typical jobs include artist, entrepreneur, designer, strategist.

There are several deeper levels of increasing complexity for measurement purposes. At the deepest level there are over 80 descriptors grouped in over 20 clusters. For example, in the *lower right* C quadrant there are six clusters. One such cluster with seven descriptors shows that I have strong thinking preferences in three of the descriptors: empathetic, people-oriented, and interpersonal.

You can access all four quadrants, and you have preferences in each quadrant. Those preferences are based on the dominance of specialised thinking processes and form the basis of The Whole Brain® Model. This in turn serves as the foundation for creating your Individual Profile.

How is an Individual Profile created?

The Herrmann Brain Dominance Instrument® (HBDI®) creates an Individual Profile. You simply complete a questionnaire online. It does not take long, and you can even save it and return later to complete it. There are no right or wrong answers. You just need to be honest with your responses.

My Individual Profile (shown opposite) shows my strength of thinking preference in each quadrant (5). Strength 3 means a low preference, which typically indicates a lack of interest in that mode of thinking. Some people may even avoid thinking in that quadrant.

Strength 2 means a secondary or intermediate preference, which represents thinking modes that are comfortable for you and available to you, as necessary.

Strength 1 means a primary or strong preference which typically indicates a quadrant where you prefer to think at work. Strength 1+ indicates a very strong preference, which can be easily sensed by your colleagues. Strengths 1 and 1+ indicate the thinking modes you prefer to use when working with others to communicate, to collaborate, to solve problems, and make decisions.

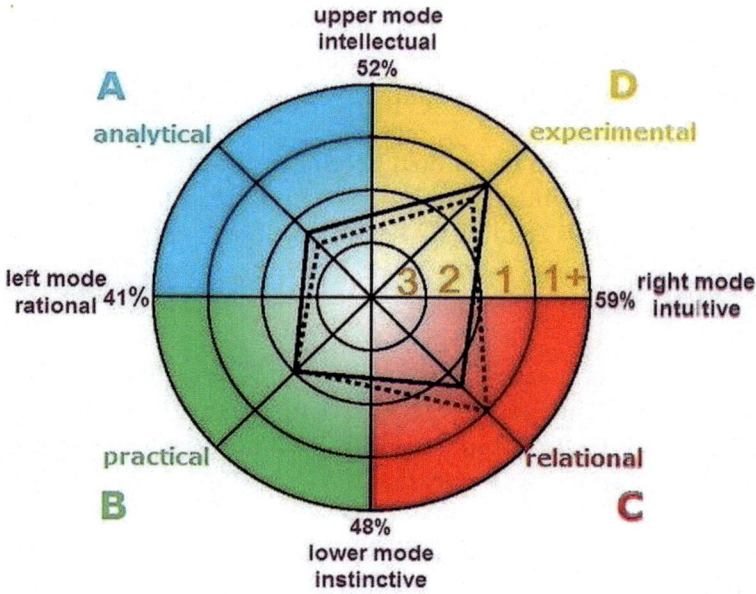

HBDI® Individual Profile 2211 for Michael Davis
The four-colour, four-quadrant graphic, and Whole Brain® are registered trademarks of Herrmann Global LLC. With kind permission of Herrmann®.

My current Individual Profile created in 2017 is summarised as 2211. Profiles are always read anti clockwise from the *upper left* A quadrant, through B and C, to D.

The dotted line shows my profile when I am thinking under pressure: I maintain the same level of practicality, whilst transferring energy from analytical and experimental thinking into relational thinking to engage with people for resolving the cause of the pressure. My profile shows that I prefer to think slightly more intellectually than instinctively (52% to 48%), and significantly more intuitively than rationally (59% to 41%).

Your Individual Profile report shows your key descriptors which reflect your thinking preferences in day-to-day life, and the work elements reflecting your thinking preferences at work. It shows the work elements you do best, and those you do least well. My profile report states that I would be most satisfied by work which includes taking risks, designing, seeing 'the big picture', being part of a team, helping people, and listening first before talking – all of which is true.

Please note that an Individual Profile code such as 2211 is just a handy and memorable summary. Each band (3, 2, 1, 1+) is actually 33 units wide. My detailed profile is A53, B63, C76, and D100. Hence you can see from the model that a very large number of profiles could be 2211.

The profile is measured in positive numbers only, outwards from zero at the centre. Hence cognitive diversity measured using the HBDI® is purely positive. Even very low scores in Strength 3 never go negative.

Profiling measures your thinking preferences, not your situational abilities. As my profile 2211 indicates, my thinking preferences at work in analytical and practical thinking are intermediate (strength 2). Yet in my domestic setting I can be very analytical and very practical. For example, I enjoyed DIY including car engine rebuilds, changing clutches, brakes, suspension, re-sprays, and maintenance; house painting inside and outside; installing kitchens, bathrooms, and cloakrooms; electrics, plumbing, tiling walls and floors, central heating, power showers, brick laying, and garden landscaping.

Researching, structuring, planning, organising, writing, illustrating, proofreading, editing, publishing, pricing, and marketing this book in Kindle and paperback versions has exercised all four quadrants.

So, with the old left-right brain model, there are only three possible profiles: left, right, or left and right. However, with four quadrants, and three strengths in each, there are a minimum of 3 x 3 x 3 x 3 = 81 possible profiles, which offers a much richer environment for development.

The profiling method is well-proven

The HBDI® was validated in 1980, and that validation still stands today. The HBDI® profiling method has been used to produce over three million Individual Profiles, in over 20 languages, in over 55 countries worldwide, in 97% of Fortune 100 companies including NASA, CISCO, PwC, Microsoft, and Mitsubishi Motors.

The profiling method is unique

The HBDI® profiling method is fact-based, brain-based, thinking-based, and is different from other popular assessment tools which are based on:

- psychology: Myers-Briggs MBTI®

- personality: Big 5, and Hogan Personality Inventory

- behaviour: DiSC®, 360°, EQ, TKI, and FIRO-B®

- talents and interests: StrengthsFinder, and Strong Interest Inventory®.

The HBDI® is also unique in being scalable on all four levels: individuals, pairs, teams, and organisations.

Cognitive Diversity At Work™ illustrated

To illustrate Cognitive Diversity At Work™, we use this graphic, which is a registered design of Cognitive Diversity Ltd:

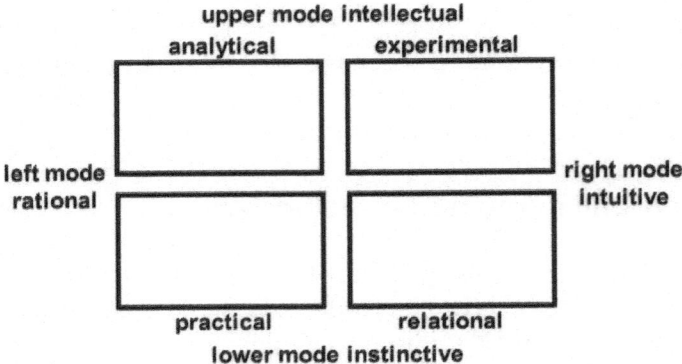

It simply and elegantly captures the essence of Whole Brain® Thinking cognitive diversity, whilst allowing space for illustrating my insights into what is really going on between people. The following case study on Individual Profile dominant thinking shows how it works.

Individual Profile dominant thinking

Having a strong thinking preference in a quadrant indicates that it is a dominant quadrant. A person will always be dominant in at least one quadrant. When the Herrmann® organisation analysed the individual profiles of more than 1.5 million adults from over 55 countries worldwide, they found that 5% had a single dominant quadrant, 58% had two dominant quadrants, 34% had three dominant quadrants, and 3% had four dominant quadrants.

Four dominant quadrants can be called a 'balanced profile'. It means that the individual can communicate, collaborate, solve problems, and make decisions naturally in all four quadrants: analytical, practical, relational, and experimental.

Many CEOs have this profile. Even without formally profiling an individual one can sense that they have a balanced profile. I believe one such person is Dr Rowan Story AM, a true polymath.

I was attending the Last Post Service at the Shrine of Remembrance late on a sunny Sunday afternoon in Melbourne, Australia. The Shrine is a magnificent and deeply moving memorial honouring the service and sacrifice of Victorians and Australians in war, peacemaking, and peacekeeping.

Photo by Michael Davis
Michael Davis with the Shrine Guard

The short service includes a testimony by a veteran or relative, bugle calls and a piper, a Shrine Guard in historic uniform, a wreath-laying, the recital of the Ode, and the lowering of the flags. Leading the service was Air Commodore Dr Rowan Story AM, RAAF.

Dr Story is an oral and maxillofacial surgeon, a lawyer teaching law and ethics to dentistry students, a volunteer at a community legal service, a member of the Victorian Civil and Administrative Tribunal, an officer of the Supreme Court of Australia, and leader of an annual volunteer surgical team to Vietnam. As an Air Commodore he was responsible for the recruitment, training, and care of all medical and health personnel in the Royal Australian Air Force.

Dr Story has said: "For a lot of people, the jobs they will be doing in the future haven't yet been invented, so it's important to be flexible and open to whatever interests you. Scientific and biological thinking is separate from legal thinking – so it forces you to think differently depending on your situation."

In saying that, Dr Story perfectly described cognitive diversity in a nutshell: the ability to think situationally, in tune with other people's different thinking styles. For all these reasons, I believe that Dr Story is a 'balanced thinker', dominant in all four quadrants:

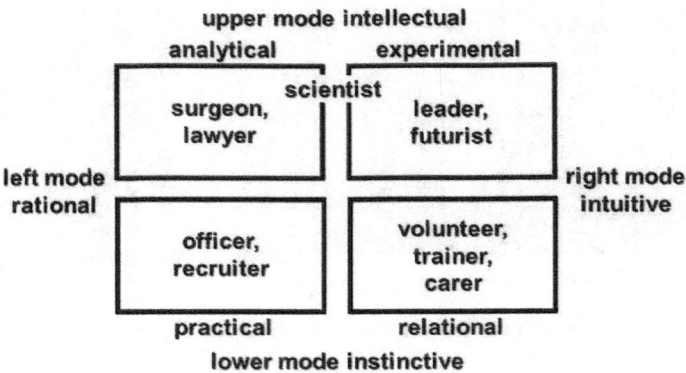

Dr Rowan Story AM: dominant in all four quadrants

Get your own Individual Profile

To get your own HBDI® Individual Profile please visit website cognitivediversity.co.uk/profiling.

For the best outcomes you can choose a private, confidential, one-to-one, facilitation feedback. This would ensure you fully understood your profile in the context of your working environment and your goals. This would be your opportunity to ask questions and seek insights. This is a premium service which can blend cognitive diversity, Neuro-Linguistic Programming, performance coaching, and mentoring, as necessary. It can be a life-changing experience – it was for me - or you can choose a general feedback in an open group setting.

For two people with the same profile code, the differences can be subtle and particularly important at the lower detailed cluster levels. For example, the 'centre of gravity' of my profile is the same as Spike Lee, the film director. I have always been fascinated in how a director imagines a film from script to screen. Making a feature film certainly is a large, costly, and complex project. It derives its complexity from the interplay between the large number of people involved, all with their individual thinking preferences.

Profiling, consultancy, and workshops

The companion website to this book shows a practical approach to profiling, consultancy, and workshops on how to deal with people, build great teams, communicate, make decisions, and solve problems.

Chapter 3. Can Your Individual Profile Change?

Your Individual Profile reflects your current thinking, which is the result of decades of nature and nurture forming your neural pathways. Over time these pathways settle and form your comfort zones.

Yet it is possible to choose new thinking and create new neural pathways and by repetition strengthen them. You can break out of your comfort zones and into new habits of thinking. These new habits eventually show up as a change in your profile. It is not possible to manipulate the online HBDI® questionnaire to get the profile that you want. Your profile reflects your thinking, not the other way round.

So, yes, your profile can change. I can show you ways of quickly strengthening any of your thinking preferences if that is your intention. My own experience shows that, without that intention, a profile change can take many years.

I estimate that my relational thinking as a young man was level 3, due to my upbringing. After marrying, my wife's influence gradually improved my relational thinking. By 2004 my first Individual Profile was 2221, and by 2017 my second profile was 2211. The significant change to my profile was in strengthening my relational thinking from 2 to 1.

It is important to state that none of the activities I describe below were undertaken with the intention of changing my profile. They were undertaken in my spare time, outside my work engaged in 'left brained' technical projects. When I saw the change in 2017, I was able to explain it using cognitive diversity as follows.

Professionally, I undertook training at my own expense and acquired new relational thinking, skills, knowledge, and experience in Whole Brain® Thinking, NLP, and Performance Coaching. At work I have always tried to help other people fulfil their true potential: it simply took time to learn how to do that professionally. Domestically, I realise that my profile also changed through relating to people outside of work more.

I took up dancing, which is very sociable and pleasurable. Learning new moves with up to 40 partners an evening is a great way to grow relational thinking.

I took up walking and volunteered to lead walks over the South Downs in support of Storrington Conservation. The walks offer health, fitness, and good conversation. At the end, we have a sociable chat over coffee and cake. I take care to ensure that my walkers safely enjoy a different walk each month, offering great views and variety of countryside.

Ray, sixth from the left in the picture below, went down very badly with COVID-19 just four days after this picture was taken. He survived, and our walks over the South Downs strengthened our mental and physical health during the pandemic. My short daily walks locally by the sea are a real tonic and set me up for the day.

Photo by Michael Davis

Some of my walkers just before the first COVID-19 lockdown

I supported my next-door neighbour for nine years until dementia forced him to enter a nursing home, where he sadly succumbed to COVID-19 aged 90.

I volunteered to help in the Day Room at St Barnabas Hospice in Worthing. The truly inspirational male nurse-in-charge had the most wonderful way of relating to adults with life-limiting conditions. I also helped with fund-raising.

When my hearing struggled with the mumblings of actors, I turned from the theatre to ballet and opera. The Royal Ballet at Covent Garden is truly a world class national treasure. Michael Powell, who with Emeric Pressburger wrote, produced and directed possibly the best of British films, said that their film *The Red Shoes* was unique because "...it was about art, and nothing but art, and nothing but the best of art." A morning art exhibition at a London gallery followed by a ballet matinee on a Saturday is a perfect celebration of right mode thinking!

I volunteered for church work. I acted as webmaster for two local churches, and now proclaim the Liturgy of the Word at Mass – 'reading the Lesson'. I take care to ensure that the congregation hear the words clearly and can make sense of them in the context of the service. This is not a performance, or a presentation, or a speech, or a lecture, or acting: it is not an easy thing to do. I am conscious that the Word is very precious to members of the congregation.

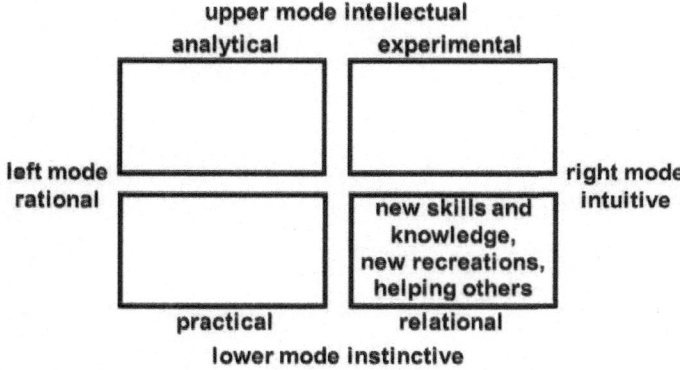

How Michael Davis grew his relational thinking

Chapter 4: End Stereotyping at Work

Men and women thinking at work

Stereotyping says that men are left-brained, women are right-brained, the left brain is male, and the right brain is female. Is this myth or reality?

Research shows that the relative numbers of men and women at work worldwide, with a dominant thinking preference quadrant by quadrant, can be illustrated as follows:

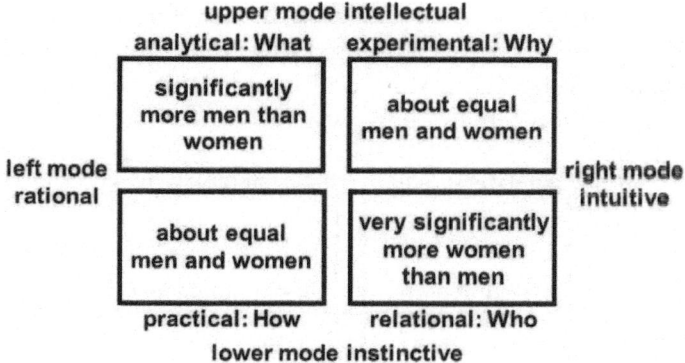

**The relative numbers of men and women
with strong thinking preferences, quadrant by quadrant**

Significantly more men than women have a strong preference for analytical thinking. Interestingly, not all men have a strong preference for analytical thinking.

About half of all men and half of all women have a strong preference for practical thinking, in approximately equal numbers.

Very significantly more women than men have a strong preference for relational thinking. Very interestingly, not all women have a strong preference for relational thinking.

About half of all men and half of all women have a strong preference for experimental thinking, in approximately equal numbers.

End the myth of stereotyping

Instead of using the traditional term 'left brained' let us combine the analytical and practical ways of thinking to form the rational left mode. This mode covers 'What will we do?' *(upper left analytical)* , and 'How will we do it?' *(lower left practical)*.

About half of all men have strong preferences in both analytical and practical thinking. However, significantly more men than women have this combination: this can explain the stereotyping of 'left-brained' as male.

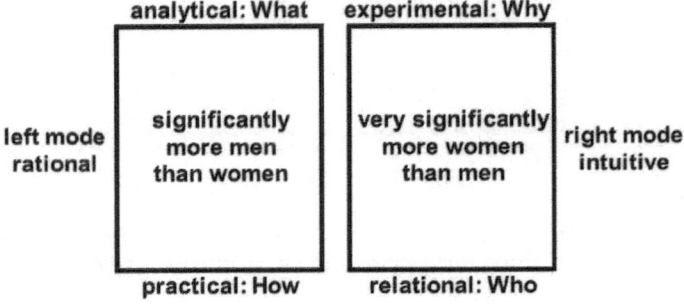

The relative numbers of men and women with strong thinking preferences in the left and right modes

Instead of using the traditional term 'right brained' let us combine the experimental *(upper right)* and relational *(lower right)* ways of thinking to form the intuitive right mode. This mode covers 'Why will we do it?' *(upper right)*, and 'Who will do it?' *(lower right)*. (The *lower left* practical thinking identifies the number of human resources that will be needed. The *lower right* relational thinking thinks of the human resources as people).

More than a third of all women have strong preferences for both experimental and relational thinking. However, very significantly more women than men have this combination: this can explain the stereotyping of 'right brained' as female. In summarising, there are men who are strongly intuitive right mode thinkers, but women very significantly outnumber them. There are women who are strongly rational left mode thinkers, but men significantly outnumber them.

We can therefore end the myths of stereotyping at work that all men are 'left-brained' and that all women are 'right-brained', and that the 'left brain' is all male and the 'right brain' is all female.

Chapter 5: End Groupthink at Work

The meaning of your communication

This chapter explores how the four ways of thinking communicate, from the most difficult to the easiest (2). It includes groupthink, which is what happens when you work only with people who think the same way you do.

NLP teaches that the meaning of your communication is the effect you are having on other people. If you do not like the effect you are having, then the onus is on you to adjust your communication until you do. The self-knowledge of your Individual Profile will greatly help you to do this.

Communication at work

Imagine a business comprising four separate functions, where the four ways of strong thinking preferences are represented by Engineering, Production, Sales, and Styling:

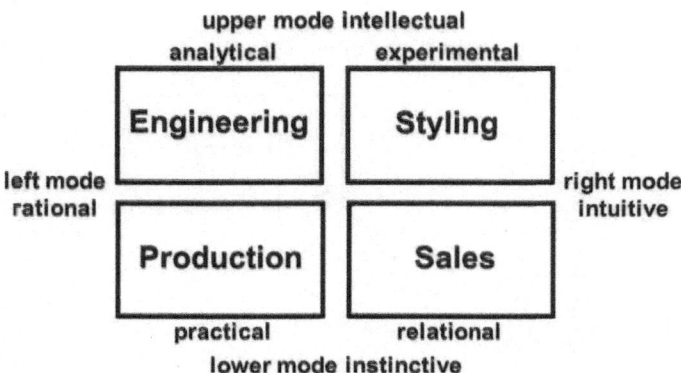

A business comprising four ways of thinking

The most difficult communication

The most difficult communication can be when Engineering work with Sales across the analytical/relational diagonal, as shown overleaf:

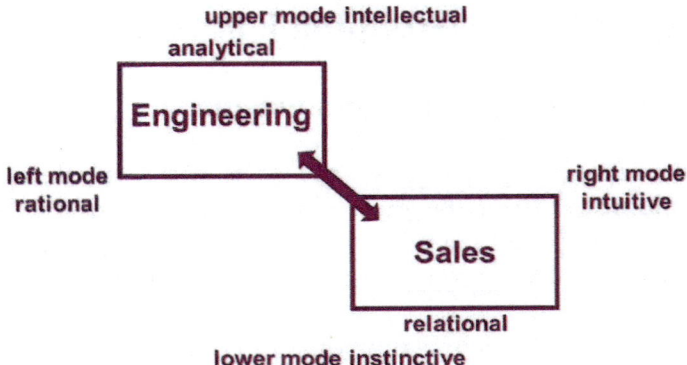

The most difficult communication of all

This is where misunderstandings and confrontation can occur because communication is crossing two boundaries: upper and lower, and left and right. There are significantly more men than women with strong analytical thinking, and very significantly more women than men with strong relational thinking.

Difficult communication

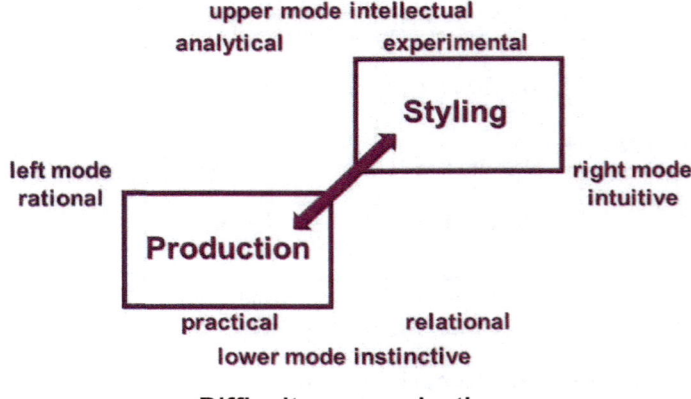

Difficult communication

Difficult communication is when Production work with Styling across the practical/experimental diagonal. There are similar numbers of men and women with strong practical thinking, and with strong experimental thinking.

Less difficult communication

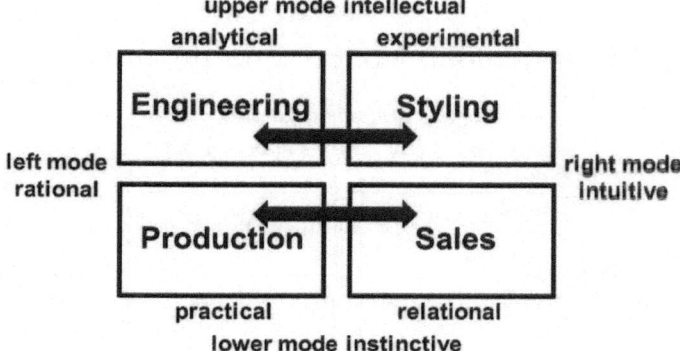

**Less difficult communication is
either intellectual or instinctive**

Workers can be in synergy, but the difference in working styles can be challenging.

Easier communication

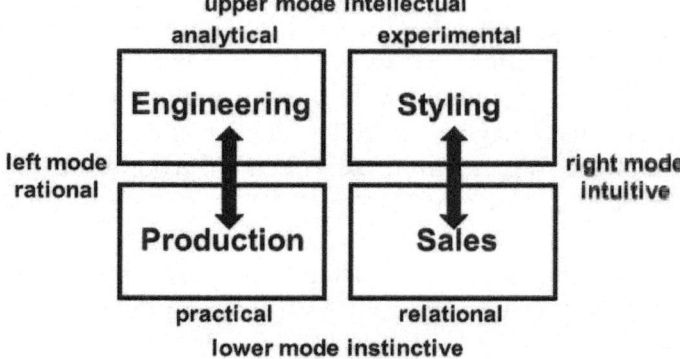

Easier communication is either rational or intuitive

Workers can be mutually supportive and sympathetic and can quickly cotton on to each other's thinking. However, this speed of communication can lead to shorthand and assumptions, and hence false understandings. I have noticed this between the design and manufacturing functions on technical projects.

The easiest communication: groupthink

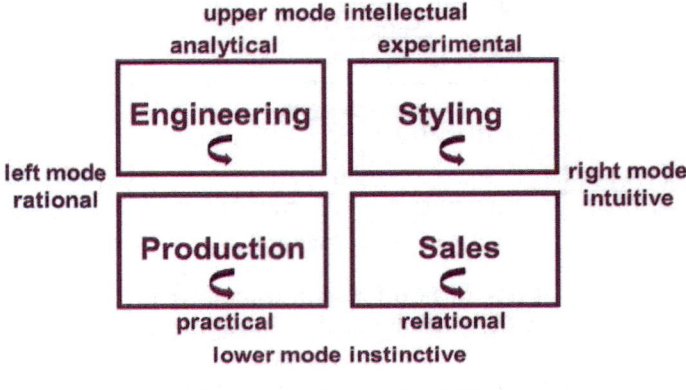

Groupthink can be tribal

This is the easiest form of communication. When the workers in a single function are communicating amongst themselves, they can be on the same wavelength, fully understanding each other, reading each other's minds, quickly solving problems and making decisions. However, this can become tribal, and groupthink can take hold. When that happens, opinions from other functions may be ignored to the detriment of the whole organisation. We examine the effects of groupthink further in Chapter 17 on COVID-19.

One of the worst cases of groupthink to my mind was the way the elite military class on both sides conducted the First World War. In 2014 I saw the deeply moving view of 888,246 ceramic poppies that filled the moat of the Tower of London, arranged by ceramic artist Paul Cummins and stage designer Tom Piper. Each poppy represented a British or colonial military death during the conflict.

The level of groupthink and killing was replicated world-wide in the combatant nations: *Wikipedia* reports up to 22 million military deaths worldwide. In his book *First World*

War (6) Martin Gilbert wrote that even as late as August 1918: 'Such was the habit of warmaking...that London, Paris and even Berlin continued to think in terms of renewed offensives, retrenchment, and the war of 1919.' However, new thinking in Berlin brought the fighting to a sudden and unforeseen end on 11 November 1918.

"Tower of London poppy shot" by Boostboy69 is licensed under CC BY 2.0

'Like a river of blood pouring from a window'

Groupthink is reported to be rife in Whitehall. Liam Halligan commented in *The Telegraph* that 'Treasury groupthink has damaged Britain for decades...Whitehall economists, while decent and hard-working, are, above all, risk averse...in return for a steady wage, and cast-iron job security, they would rather be precisely wrong than roughly right.'

Liz Truss, a former Chief Secretary to the Treasury, has said that the Treasury has an economic orthodoxy, resists change, and has been peddling a particular type of economic policy for 20 years which hasn't delivered growth. Being risk-averse reflects *lower left* thinking.

End the blindness of groupthink at work

Groupthink at work can result in rapid problem-solving, decision-making, and communication. Whether the solutions or decisions make sense to all other thinkers in the organisation is another matter. To quote Professor Margaret Heffernan, groupthink can also be bad through '...internally generated blindness that leaves institutions exposed and out of touch'.

An organisation that seems to eschew groupthink is GCHQ, the world class UK Government Communications Headquarters. Sir Jeremy Fleming, when Director of GCHQ, said: "...we look back on a history of amazing intelligence, world-leading innovation, and the ingenious people...it's a history defined by the belief that with the right mix of minds, anything is possible."

The four values of GCHQ are Integrity, Impact, Teamwork, and Ingenuity. Cognitive Diversity At Work™ places these values broadly in analytical, practical, relational, and experimental thinking, respectively. To achieve the right mix of minds, GCHQ will be practising cognitive diversity by drawing on very strong thinking preferences in all four ways of thinking.

Chapter 6: Male and Female Brains

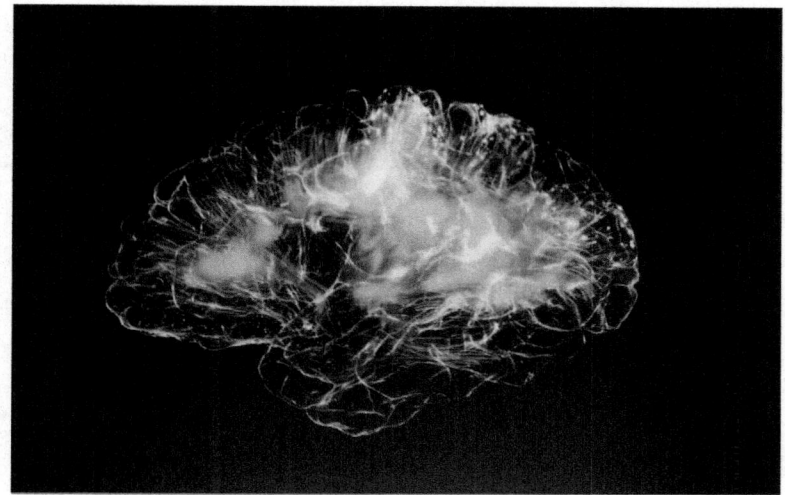

Photo by Alina Grubnyak on Unsplash

'Brains are a mixed bag'

Chapter 4 showed that significantly more men than women have a strong preference for *upper left* analytical thinking, and very significantly more women than men have a strong preference for *lower right* relational thinking.

Does this mean that there are separate 'male' and 'female' brains anatomically? Or does it mean that there is a common anatomical brain with either a 'left' or 'right' bias? We need to look at two cases of research into the anatomical brain.

Gina Rippon, Professor of Neuroimaging at Aston University, has said: "…the concept of a 'male' and 'female' brain is flawed…every brain is actually a mosaic of different patterns, some more commonly found in men's brains and some in women's…many of the psychological traits we think of as either male or female actually exist on a spectrum…a study showed that behavioural characteristics do not fall into two neat, non-overlapping binary categories."

Let's just remind ourselves that the HBDI® profiling method is about thinking and not psychology or behaviour.

Aston University's findings are supported by separate research in Israel led by Daphna Joel of Tel-Aviv University. Professor Joel's researchers used MRI scans of more than 1,400 brains, focusing on anatomy rather than on how brains work.

They found that while specific parts of the brain show sex differences, an individual brain rarely has all 'male' traits or all 'female' traits and instead it is more likely to be a mixed bag – some things are more common in women, some things are more common in men, and some are common to both.

In terms of physical structure, the brains of men and women have always appeared to be identical - until now. New research on the structures of the brain at Stanford University has shown for the first time that the brains of men and women do differ structurally. The findings were published in the Proceedings of the National Academy of Sciences of the USA.

Dr Vinod Menon, professor of psychiatry and behavioural sciences at Stanford, said: "This is a very strong piece of evidence that sex is a robust determinant of human brain organisation." For the record, Ned Herrmann believed that the thinking of mature adults was based on 30% nature (male sex or female sex) and 70% nurture.

The Stanford research tool used Artificial Intelligence. It was shown MRI scans of working brains and told whether it was looking at the brain of a woman or of a man. Over time, the tool learned to pick out subtle structural differences between male and female brains that had been missed by humans. When the researchers tested the tool on some 1,500 brain scans, it was able to identify the sex of each brain with more than 90 per cent accuracy.

Dr Rippon commented: "The really intriguing issue is that those areas of the brain which are most reliably distinguishing the sexes are key parts of the social brain." This supports Chapter 4's statement that very significantly more women than men have strong relational thinking preferences.

'Men and women see things differently'

Since vision is arguably the most powerful of all our senses, are the brains of men and women different in the way they respond to visual cues?

A survey of motoring memories was commissioned to mark the start of the 30th series of the BBC's *Top Gear*. The most common memory over the past 40 years was: 'The unfurling of maps and arguments between parents over directions.' It seems that men and women do indeed use different navigation strategies.

The Norwegian University of Science and Technology has carried out formal academic research into the subject. According to lead researcher Dr Carl Pintzka, men in general use cardinal directions *(analytical thinking)* and women in general use relationships *(relational thinking)*.

For example, Dr Pintzka found that men think in terms of north, south, east, and west: the cardinal points of a compass. If the destination is in a particular direction, it matters less where you start from. This is an *upper left* logical and analytical approach.

For example, I was once lost in a wood whilst reconnoitring a walk. Tired, hungry, and thirsty I decided to simply head east whatever the obstacle – dense undergrowth, thorn bushes, or barbed wire fences - until I reached a main road that I knew would lead me back to the carpark.

Dr Pintzka found that women usually orient themselves along a route from a known starting point, joining up landmarks which they relate to. Perhaps starting at the pharmacy, then right at the post office, turning left at the bus stop and so on. This is a *lower right* relational approach. It works, because I rely on my wife to find my wallet, phone, glasses or whatever at home!

A study published in the *Journal of Vision* supports Dr Pintzka's theory: in prehistoric times, when men hunted moving prey and kept predators at a distance, they did not require a detailed view. Whereas when women gathered static objects (such as wild berries and fungi for cooking), they took great care and paid attention to detail, to avoid poisoning the family.

Isabella Mareschal, co-author of the study, said: "There are numerous claims in popular culture that women and men look at things differently - this is the first demonstration, using eye tracking, to support the claim that women take in visual information in different ways from men."

The study concluded that men and women do indeed see things differently. Evidently, women focus more on left sided facial features and have a strong left eye bias. Women also spend more time exploring a person's face, suggesting that women maintain more eye contact during conversations than men. This is a behaviour linked to relational thinking and is part of building rapport, which is of vital importance in coaching, counselling, and NLP.

In fact, researchers were able to establish the sex of participants from eye movement alone with 80% accuracy, independent of culture, since nearly 60 nationalities were tested. The study also suggested that sex difference in scanning visual information may impact many fields, such as autism diagnosis or even everyday behaviours such as watching a movie or looking at the road whilst driving.

Chapter 7: Empathy, Sympathy, and Productivity

Photo by Birmingham Museums Trust on Unsplash

Empathy and sympathy at work

Empathy means to feel *(pathos)* with others *(em)*. Philosopher Julian Baggini has stated: 'Psychologists distinguish between affective empathy, based on feeling, and cognitive empathy, which is more an intellectual understanding of how others think and feel.

'With cognitive empathy we are more able to understand what we may not feel: it can therefore be considered a more powerful tool and more accurate. Unfortunately advocates of empathy focus too much on feeling and not enough on thinking…understanding others requires head as well as heart, working out what is the right thing to do even more so. When feeling others' pain becomes everything then it not only ceases to help us do the right thing right, but it also starts to hinder us.'

As a performance coach I concur with Baggini. I have some affective empathy to the feelings or emotions of my clients, but I cannot share them fully. I am no use to my clients if I am in the same negative states as them. A coach must always be in a positive state to facilitate the change clients desire, by doing the right things right. This is why I do not recommend self-coaching. It is very difficult to be totally detached from one's own emotional state.

I equate affective empathy with *lower right* relational thinking. On reflection, I conclude that cognitive empathy is a judicious blend of fact, analysis, logic *(upper left)* and taking a strategic, holistic, and intuitive overview *(upper right)*. Hence, I equate cognitive empathy with *upper mode* intellectual thinking

Where does sympathy fit in? According to Tom Bawden, Science Correspondent of *The Independent* newspaper, 'Sympathy is being sorry for someone's misfortune and wishing them well. Which is not the same as taking on someone else's perspective so that you feel a reflection of what they feel'. So, I conclude that sympathy is more akin to *upper mode* intellectual cognitive empathy.

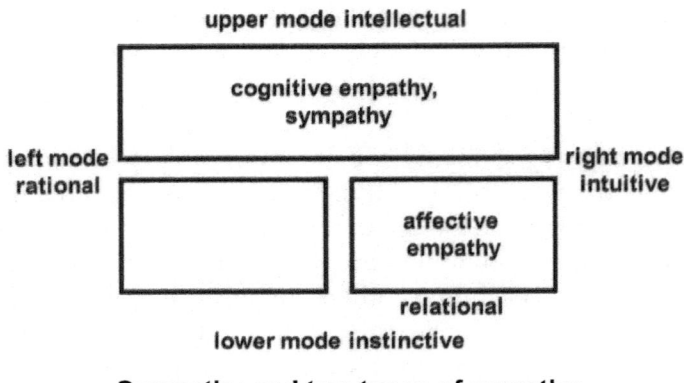

Sympathy and two types of empathy

At work, you may find yourself dealing with a colleague who is in a very emotional state. You will naturally have some measure of *lower right* affective empathy and may feel some emotion and possibly shock. Your colleague may be happy just to be listened to and their story heard.

The impulse to rush to a 'solution to their problem' is best resisted. If action is required, you can use *upper mode* intellectual cognitive empathy to jointly plan a way forward and have the sympathy to find the right words.

Productivity at work

Productivity is a crucial factor in economic performance. What is productivity, and why is improving it important?
An internationally agreed definition of national productivity is Gross Domestic Product (GDP) per hour worked. The data for calculating national productivity is sourced from the International Monetary Fund (IMF) and the Organisation for Economic Co-operation and Development (OECD).

Improving national productivity is important because more real income improves people's ability to purchase goods and services, enjoy more leisure, improve the quality of housing and education, and contribute to social and environmental initiatives, thereby raising living standards. Unfortunately, OECD data shows that UK national productivity has grown very little since 2000.

If low national productivity is seen as a problem, can Cognitive Diversity At Work™ help? Yes, it can, by addressing the problem in each of the four ways of thinking. For example, let's briefly look at how *lower right* relational thinking can help.

Productivity can be improved by increasing skills through training, and knowledge through education, and also by improving verbal and written communication so that people collaborate, solve problems, and make decisions quicker and better. Training, knowledge, and communication all reflect *lower right* relational thinking.

Productivity can also be improved by employing certain traits. A study by Exeter University published in the *Journal of Occupational and Organisational Psychology* showed a direct link between certain traits and increased productivity. The study found that companies would do well to tailor training and recruitment measures to encourage managers who have empathy, integrity and are trustworthy – as these traits can improve productivity.

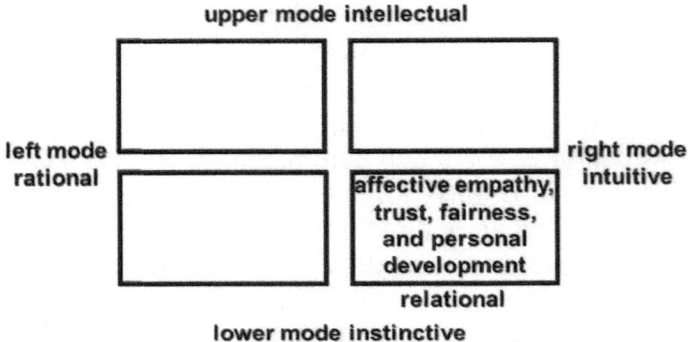

Traits linked to improving productivity

Such managers create a positive culture of trust and fairness in the workplace; in turn, they create loyal and positive teams. This type of manager is keen to encourage staff development. Affective empathy, trust, fairness, and personal development all reflect *lower right* relational thinking.

Dr Allan Lee, lead author of the Exeter report, stated: "Our work shows that a 'servant-leader' style of management which is ethical, trustworthy and has a real interest in the wellbeing and development of staff brings about real positives." In the quest for increased productivity and profitability, step forward the manager who has strong preferences in *lower right* relational thinking!

Chapter 8: Job Satisfaction

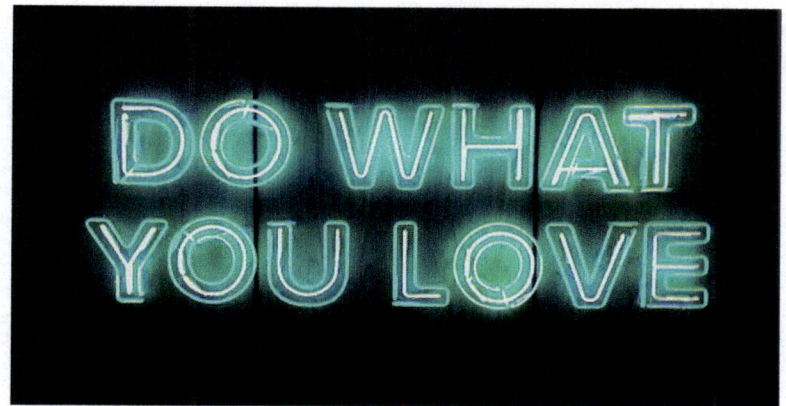

Maximising job satisfaction

You will realise intuitively that maximum job satisfaction will be found in doing work that aligns with your thinking preferences. Conversely, you will have little if any job satisfaction in work that is totally at variance with your thinking preferences.

The UK Office for National Statistics (ONS) have interesting statistics telling the story of young people starting out on their careers.

What's important to young job seekers

The ONS asked 16-to-21-year-olds which aspects were very important to them in choosing their future jobs.

72% said that that the job must be interesting. This can be assured naturally if the job holder's own primary thinking preferences are closely aligned with the job's profile.

60% said the job must be secure, which is aligned to *lower left* practical thinking in terms of liking control and aversion to risk.

40% chose 'time for the family' and 26% chose 'helping others', which are clearly aligned with *lower right* relational thinking.

Only 25% selected high income. I suspect that the 25% have primary thinking preferences in *upper left* analytical thinking.

20% selected 'contributing to society' which I link with *lower right* relational thinking.

Leaving aside the desire for their jobs to be interesting (which would mean alignment with any dominant thinking preference), the overall balance is in favour of jobs reflecting *lower right* relational thinking.

Top five jobs desired

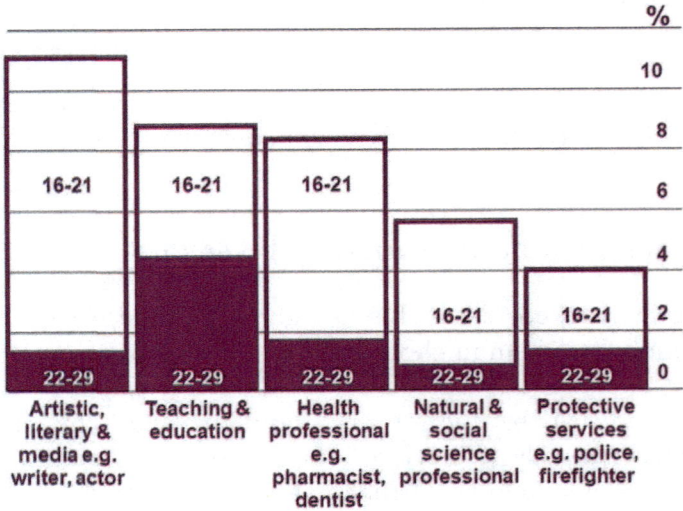

The top five jobs: aspiration in 2011-2012,
and reality in 2017

The ONS surveyed the top five jobs desired by 16-to-21-year-olds in 2011-2012, and the percentages of 22-to-29-year-olds doing those jobs in 2017 (7). They were not the same samples of people, but the ONS have assured me that the samples fairly represented the age groups at the time, so that each group could be considered to represent the same type of people.

11.22% aspired to jobs with *upper right* experimental thinking such as artistic, literary or media; only 1.39% were actually doing those jobs in 2017.

8.76% aspired to jobs with *lower right* relational thinking such as teacher or educator; 4.48% were actually doing those jobs in 2017.

A total of 13.62% aspired to jobs with *upper left* analytical thinking: health professionals such as dentist or pharmacist, and natural and social science professionals, but only 2.43% were actually doing those jobs in 2017.

Whilst 4.04% aspired to jobs with *lower left* practical thinking in protective services such as police officer or firefighter, only 1.36% were actually doing those jobs in 2017.

Only in the teaching and education jobs reflecting *lower right* thinking was there anything approaching a correlation between aspiration and outcome. I would recommend that research is carried out to test if applicants' thinking preferences are sufficiently closely aligned with job requirements. Are young people aware of the actual demands of the jobs they aspire to?

For example, I would suggest that the high drop-out rates in the glamour sectors of writing and acting reflect saturated markets, poor luck, very high competition, and maybe even a lack of talent. In dentistry, pharmacy, and social sciences, maybe the depth of the technical requirements comes as something of a shock.

A real learning point is that cognitive diversity Individual Profiling is not intended for young, pre-work people. It is intended for adults with some years of experience in the world of work. The HBDI® is not intended to be taken by young, pre-work people.

Top five jobs actually performed

Lastly, we come to the top five jobs that 22-to-29-year-olds actually performed in 2017 (7).

4.48% Teaching and Educational Professionals.
3.73% Sales, Marketing and Related Associate.
2.83% Information Technology and Telecommunications.
2.79% Childcare and Related Personal Services.
2.67% Administrative Occupations: Finance.

Cognitive Diversity At Work™ says that three job areas – teaching, sales, and childcare - align with *lower right* relational thinking. Two other areas – IT and finance – reflect *upper left* analytical thinking. The data illustrates the contrast along the *upper left–lower right* diagonal. Further analysis of the data comparing men and women could prove interesting.

Check your job satisfaction

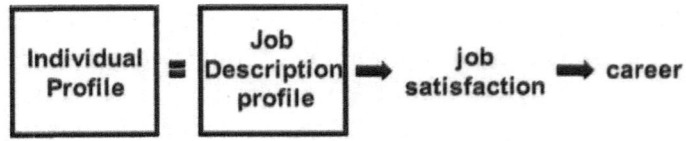

Highest job satisfaction and career prospects are when your job profile matches your thinking preferences

On cognitivediversity.co.uk/profiling we can construct a profile of your job from your detailed job description. We can then report on how your Individual Profile compares or contrasts with your job profile. The report would explain any variances between the profiles and explain the options open to you. The nearer your job description profile matches your cognitive diversity Individual Profile, the higher your job satisfaction and hence your performance in pursuing your career.

Chapter 9: Social Mobility

Photo by Ian Schneider on Unsplash

The privilege gap and social mobility

The UK Social Mobility Commission has stated that inequality is entrenched in the UK from birth to work. It found that being born privileged (high income) means you usually remain privileged (8). Being born underprivileged (poor) means you usually remain underprivileged. Hence the 'privilege gap' at work.

The Commission found that children who are born poor are only 20% likely to end up in a 'professional' job, hence the low rate of social mobility. I was one of the poor 20% and I know the passion, drive, will-power, and determination to succeed that you need to be upwardly socially mobile and secure a prestigious 'professional' job.

The key to my success was the transformative power of education. I will always be grateful to the ratepayers of Bradford who funded my degree at Imperial College, which is currently second only to the Massachusetts Institute of Technology in the world rankings of universities.

I believe that a true test of social mobility is when a child of one of the poor 20% becomes one of the affluent 80%. In other words, social mobility becomes established in the succeeding generations. I have seen this myself in my sons who are enjoying very successful international careers in software.

I wonder if the UK Social Mobility Commission is in danger of equating status with money. The Commission seems to think that bridging the privilege gap means moving from a non-professional job to a professional job. As we know, there are many non-professional jobs, such driving trains, paying far more than some professional jobs. Would moving from a high income non-professional job to a lower income professional job be regarded by the Commission as a privilege?

How can cognitive diversity help social mobility?

The Social Mobility Commission sets two questions when asking if 'something' can contribute to social mobility. The first question asks if any part of the 'something' is denied to the poor. So, is any part of cognitive diversity denied to the poor? The answer must be 'No', since all brains, rich or poor, worldwide, have access to analytical, practical, relational, and experimental thinking.

The cognitive diversity Individual Profiles of a lathe operator and a production director could be very similar. Other factors come into play that determine whether one becomes a lathe operator or a production director – and a lathe operator could well be very happy with their lot in life, thank you.

That goes for plumbers, carpenters, electricians, bricklayers, plasterers, builders, glaziers, lorry drivers, train drivers and so on. They are workers who directly add real value, and who are not accounted for as indirect managerial overheads. The second question looks for any part of the 'something' that can be correlated with success and upward social mobility. So, is there any part of cognitive diversity that can be correlated with success and upward social mobility?

As Brian Tracy the personal development guru said: "The secret to success in life is the ability to get along with other people." And Marcel Schwantes reported that: 'Microsoft co-founder Bill Gates cites the importance of personal relationships as a critical measure of his success.'

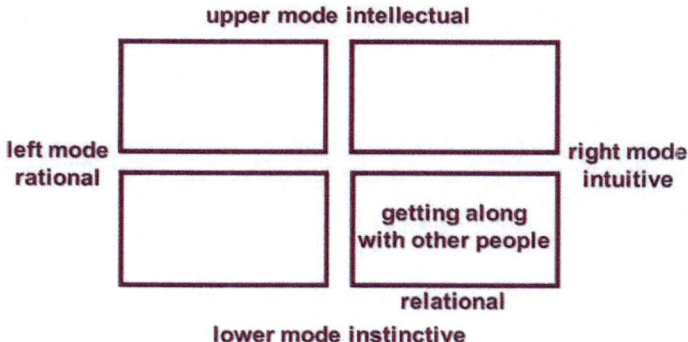

Relational thinking is a key to success in life

Schwantes also referenced the Harvard University study started in 1938 that tracked the health of 724 men in the hope of finding the clues to leading a healthy and happy life. In 2017 the Harvard study revealed that: 'Close relationships, more than money or fame, are what keep people happy throughout their lives. 'Those ties protect people from life's discontents, help to delay mental and physical decline, and are better predictors of long and happy lives than social class, IQ, or even genes.'

Dr Anna Machin, an evolutionary anthropologist, said: "The relationships you have are the number one factor in your mental and physical health and your longevity. Friendships are incredibly important, so are family and community". So, the part of cognitive diversity that can be correlated with success and upward social mobility is *lower right* relational thinking.

Chapter 10: Directors, and Entrepreneurs

Photo by Danielle Cerullo on Unsplash

Emotional intelligence in the boardroom

In 2010, 12.5% of directors of UK FTSE 100 boards were women. That year, Dame Helena Morrissey DBE established the 30% Club with the target of raising that number to 30% by 2015 (9). She wrote at the time: 'Leaders, we now know, need to be emotionally intelligent.' The inference seemed to be that only women could bring emotional intelligence to boardrooms.

The 30% target was reached in September 2018, and the percentage in 2024 is almost 40%. The 30% Club is now a global campaign with 18 Chapters worldwide.

The club believes that 'only those organisations that foster truly inclusive cultures - cultures that embrace women who look, act and, importantly, THINK differently - can reach their full potential to positively impact their people, their markets, and their communities'.

Let us look at the statement on 'emotional intelligence'. Chapter 7 shows that emotional intelligence is linked with affective empathy, which is linked with *lower right* relational thinking. Chapter 4 shows that very significantly more women than men have a strong preference in relational thinking.

Yet a female candidate for the board may be one of the women who do not have a strong preference in *lower right* relational thinking. On the other hand, a male candidate for the board may be one of the men who do have a strong preference in *lower right* relational thinking. So, it seems that simply imposing a quota by itself will not automatically guarantee an increase in emotional intelligence.

Let us now look at the statement on 'truly inclusive cultures'. Chapter 1 shows that Cognitive Diversity At Work™ fully satisfies the definition of inclusion set by Abbott Laboratories (3).

If the board is balanced 50% men and 50% women, then there is a better chance of all four ways of thinking being represented strongly. Ned Herrmann found that heterogeneous teams – 50% men and 50% women, outperform homogeneous teams - 100% men or 100% women.

Dame Helena has also written: 'Men and women can be equal but stay different.' Yes, even if a man and a woman have the same cognitive diversity Individual Profile, there are ways in which they will stay different! But those ways, such as femininity and masculinity, are outside the scope of this book…

Are entrepreneurs male only?

Dr Lianne Taylor wrote in *The Conversation* that: '…in popular thinking around entrepreneurship, certain attributes are presented as male-only (10). These traits include self-esteem, risk-taking, autonomous decision-making, over-confidence, the need for control, resilience, and ego. Put all that together and you have a familiar archetype…of the male entrepreneur. The trouble is that female entrepreneurship is commonly described in opposite to these traits.' What does Cognitive Diversity At Work™ have to say on the matter?

Dr Taylor's list of traits is a mix of masculine traits such as self-esteem, autonomous decision-making, over confidence, resilience and ego, and the thinking preferences of controlling and of risk taking. We shall focus on the thinking preferences.

A study by Huefner, Hunt, and Robinson (11) found that all entrepreneurs, whether male or female, have strong or very strong preferences in what we call *upper right* experimental thinking.

There are two types of entrepreneur: technical and non-technical entrepreneurs. Let's look first at technical entrepreneurs. Herrmann found that technical entrepreneurs, whether male or female, have strong preferences in analytical thinking and in experimental thinking. In the illustration below I have omitted practical and relational thinking preferences.

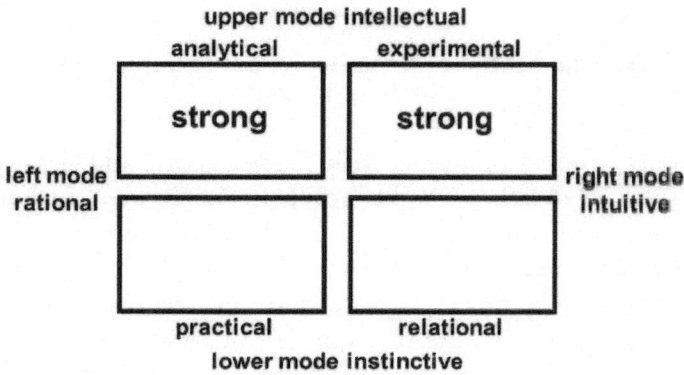

Typical profile of a technical entrepreneur, male or female

If it seems there are more male technical entrepreneurs than female it is simply because there are significantly more males than females with strong preferences in analytical thinking.

Herrmann found that non-technical entrepreneurs, whether male or female, have strong or very strong preferences in both relational *(lower right)* and experimental *(upper right)* thinking. If it seems there are more female non-technical entrepreneurs than male, it is simply because there are very significantly more females than males with strong preferences in relational thinking. In the illustration below I have omitted analytical and practical thinking preferences.

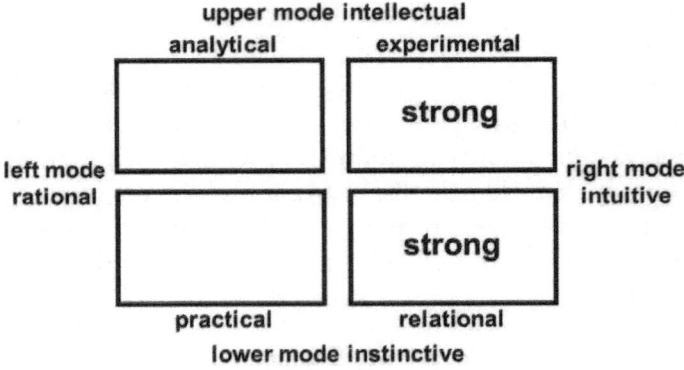

Typical profile of a non-technical entrepreneur, male or female

All entrepreneurs embrace risk *(upper right)* and have low interest in detail or tight control *(lower left practical)*. Experimental thinking is most useful in the start-up, infancy, and risky adolescence of an enterprise. However, if an enterprise is to grow, mature and survive, then practical thinking needs to come to the fore – otherwise constant risk taking can destroy it.

Serial entrepreneurs are therefore characterised by starting up and quickly selling businesses and moving on to their next big idea. As the flamboyant billionaire financier and tycoon Sir James Goldsmith said: "If you see a bandwagon, it's too late." True entrepreneurs create bandwagons and then jump off to start new ones rolling.

So, technical entrepreneurs and non-technical entrepreneurs can be either male or female. Cognitive diversity shows why there seem to be more male technical entrepreneurs, and why there seem to be more female non-technical entrepreneurs.

Chapter 11: Men and Relational Thinking

Acknowledgement: Sands United

Some men can struggle to talk

Sands – the Stillbirth and Neonatal Death Society - is a leading stillbirth and neonatal death charity in the UK (12). According to Sands, babies dying is not rare and every 90 minutes in the UK a baby dies shortly before, during, or soon after birth.

I will never forget the terrible labour my dear wife experienced with our second son. It was a ghastly nightmare. He was eventually delivered by emergency Caesarean section, 'flat' but alive. I thought I had lost them both. I cannot bear to think of the alternative outcome.

Sands knows that when a baby dies the feelings of loneliness and isolation can be overwhelming for all concerned and having other bereaved parents to talk to is vital. However, Sands knows that fathers can sometimes be overlooked or struggle to find ways of getting support that suits them. The charity knows that some men can struggle to talk about how they are feeling after the death of a baby.

Sands found a method for men to get support that suits men. 90 minutes also happens to be the duration of a football match. So, men formed football teams called Sands United based on existing football grounds around the country. I count 42 teams so far, and the nearest to my home is Sands United FC Brighton and Hove.

Sands believes that the football clubs are a unique way for fathers - and other bereaved family members – to come together through a shared love of sport and find a support network. Somewhere fathers can feel at ease and talk about their grief when they are ready to. The fathers also commemorate their babies by proudly displaying their names on the football kit worn for every match.

Sands believes that playing team sports can aid the grieving process by helping lift someone's mood, giving them a focus, helping with sleep problems, and reducing feelings of isolation. Sands also believes that the teams have saved the lives of men from suicide who felt like they had no one to turn to in their grief.

The learning point is that having a low preference for, or avoiding, *lower right* relational thinking can be harmful for your wellbeing. Chapter 4 shows that men are more likely than women to be in that situation. The knack is finding a setting, such as Sands, in which men can grow their relational thinking.

'Men tend to be solitary'

Another setting in which men can grow their relational thinking is the Men's Pie Club. There some 19 clubs spread around Newcastle and Leeds. A member of the Byker club in Newcastle was quoted as saying: "Women like to talk to other women and interact more, while men tend to be solitary. When they are on their own, men think: 'Maybe I'll have a pint'. They never think of an alternative beyond a drink of alcohol. Men don't tend to interact with other men, and Pie Club brings men together, and we feel like we have known each other a long time."

The Pie Club is run by Food Nation and brings men together as an antidote to social isolation and to improve their mental health. Over couple of hours, the men make their own meat pies from raw ingredients and chat whilst doing so.

In the old days of full employment in heavy engineering, men in the Northeast of England had plenty of opportunity for banter at work and in the social clubs. Sadly, in our post-industrial society, that is no longer the case. In a traditional culture where 'boys don't cry', the 'stiff upper lip' stiffens even more, and men 'man up', social isolation can have devastating results. The Northeast of England has suffered the highest rate of male suicide in the country. The Men's Pie Club is another successful way for men to grow their relational thinking.

Male reporters called 'emotional retards'

There is anecdotal evidence that some women regard men as emotionless number crunchers. On 14 June 2017, a fire broke out in the 24-storey Grenfell Tower block of flats in North Kensington, West London. 72 residents died, more than 70 others were injured, and 223 people escaped. It was the deadliest structural fire in the United Kingdom since the 1988 Piper Alpha oil rig disaster and the worst UK residential fire since the Second World War.

The fire was started by a malfunctioning fridge-freezer on the fourth floor. It rapidly spread up the building's exterior, bringing fire and smoke to all the residential floors. The rapid spread has been attributed to both the building's cladding and the external insulation.

The fire burned for about 60 hours before finally being extinguished. More than 250 London Fire Brigade firefighters and 70 fire engines fought to control the fire and rescue residents. More than 100 London Ambulance Service crews and at least 20 ambulances attended, joined by specialist paramedics from the Ambulance Service's Hazardous Area

Response Team. The Metropolitan Police and London's Air Ambulance also assisted the rescue effort. This grim story has been outlined to set the scene for how the tragedy was reported.

British journalist and author Yasmin Alibhai-Brown wrote that when she spoke to local women after the fire, they said that most of the male reporters were only interested in numbers and bare facts *(strong upper left analytical thinking)*.

Women called the male reporters '...emotional retards, effing robots who didn't get the real story' *(avoiding lower right relational thinking)*. Alibhai-Brown wrote that the male reporters do get the story but can only tell it in formulaic *(upper left)* ways.

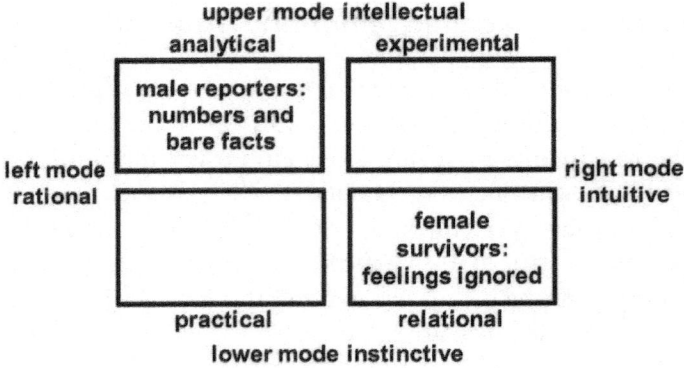

How female survivors felt about most of the male reporting of the Grenfell fire

Perhaps there is a case here for male reporters to be trained to reflect relational thinking in their reports, and for editors to expect it.

Chapter 12: Letting Agents Anger Tenants

What Whaley Bridge could have looked like

An example of most difficult communication

Chapter 5 shows that communication is most difficult across the *upper left analytical/ lower right relational* diagonal. An outstanding example of this was to be found in the way local letting agents warned tenants that they may not be insured for flooding.

As we know, insurance is based on actuarial calculations *(upper left)* of a risk *(lower left)*, the premium to be paid, and the financial compensation *(upper left)* to be paid out if the risk occurs. House and contents insurance documents run to many pages of terms and conditions *(lower left)*. It is a prudent renter of a property who makes sure that their contents are fully insured.

This brings us to Whaley Bridge in Derbyshire which found itself under the threat of flooding due to the possible failure of the 150-year dam at Toddbrook Reservoir. In August 2019, 1,500 residents and people in nearby Furness Vale and New Mills were evacuated on the orders of police. The

Royal Air Force were drafted in, with Chinook helicopters providing support and dropping aggregate to bolster the dam.

Worried about losing life, possessions, and home from 300 million gallons of water rushing through the town, possibly the last thing people expected was an email message from local letting agents.

The agents were offering insurance quotes and warning some types of insurance would mean tenants were not covered. The agency thought they were being helpful, but the communication backfired, and the response was one of anger by some tenants.

One tenant said: "I felt it was an attempt to make money *(upper left)*. I thought it was an insensitive and insulting thing to do *(avoiding lower right)*. It seems like they have no concern for my family, my friends, and the people of Whaley Bridge *(avoiding lower right)* and the fact that their lives are in danger. But if you make a bit of commission on insurance sales, then – terrific!"

Another tenant asked: "Is that a joke? What about the email you sent round trying to sell us insurance *(upper left)* and never once asking if we were safe *(avoiding lower right)*?"

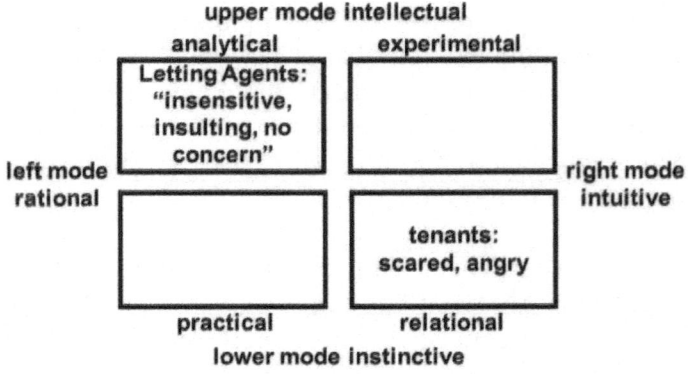

How tenants felt about the communication

64

'We should have been more empathetic.'

The agents subsequently admitted they could have handled the situation differently, but also said some clients had been pleased to get the email. They issued the following statement: 'With severe flood warnings in place across areas of the Northwest and with the protection of our tenants' belongings in mind, we sent out an email to all of our tenants on the morning of Thursday to remind them that they needed to have their own insurance in place to cover their personal belongings.'

The statement continued: 'Following the email we have had over 50 responses from tenants who did not have the appropriate insurance in place, thanking us for drawing their attention to this. We have supported these clients and helped them to insure their household belongings. Given the unfolding of events in Whaley Bridge and the distress people in areas such as Poynton were experiencing, we accept our communication should have been more empathetic *(lower right).'*

The statement ended with 'We do, however, stand by our actions in sending out the communication. Our thoughts are with the communities impacted by these events; indeed, we are very much part of these communities and are working with clients in these areas to support them *(lower right)* during this difficult time.'

So, the letting agents' intentions were good, they had the best interests of their community at heart, and they admitted the email could have been better. The key phrase is, '...our communication should have been more empathetic.'

Unfortunately, from the tenants' relational thinking point of view, the email from the agents was interpreted as an insensitive attempt at drumming up business at the last minute in an already stressful situation. There is no right or wrong judgement here: simply different ways of thinking.

Full marks to the letting agents for realising that organisations need to make their communications more attuned to their audience, whatever the circumstances. It is not an easy thing to do, especially when under pressure. The cognitive diversity Individual Profile shows how your thinking changes when you are under pressure and stressed.

Chapter 13: Cognitive Diversity in the Law

Lady Justice at the Old Bailey

The next three chapters give a few examples of cognitive diversity in the law, in health, and in education. Readers are invited to send examples from their own experience to md@cognitivediversity.co.uk, for my analysis and comment.

Trial left a family 'a smoking wreck'

To relational thinkers, analytical thinkers such as lawyers can appear cold, rigid, ruthless, calculating, short term, and always needing proof. To analytical thinkers such as lawyers, relational thinkers can appear un–business–like, over sensitive, sentimental, and emotional. This was starkly illustrated at the trial of serial killer Levi Bellfield for the murder of Milly Dowler.

In her book *My Sister Milly,* Gemma Dowler described the behaviour of Bellfield's defence lawyer, the justice system, and the police (13). It is a deeply distressing, harrowing, and disturbing account of how the law can appear to an innocent family still grieving for their murdered child. Time and again

I had to put the book down and return to it later when my anger subsided.

An editorial in *The Mail on Sunday:* stated: 'Bellfield's QC, having no proper evidence to offer and hampered by his client's guilty silence, chose to attack Milly's parents. This was a distressing, pointless exhibition. Bellfield was already in prison for two other murders. His liberty was not at stake, and he had no reputation to lose.'

Fiona McIntosh wrote in the *Sunday Mirror:* 'That monster Bellfield murdered Milly, and the justice system did its best to murder what was left of her grieving family. It subjected the Dowlers to relentless mental torture. It left a young woman emotionally scarred for life and pushed her mother to the brink of insanity. The trial of Bellfield has left the family a smoking wreck.'

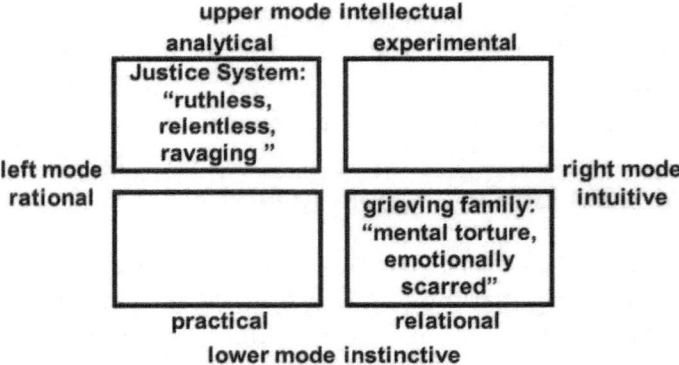

'The trial left a family a smoking wreck'

Dame Louise Casey, who has served both as the government's neighbourhood crime adviser and as the Victims' Commissioner, said: "It is time the system takes a look at itself. If the message is 'Do not go into a courtroom because you will be ravaged, your entire life will be torn apart, that people go too far, all in order to ensure due process for the defendant' – then I think a wake-up call needs to happen."

Sir Keir Starmer KC, who was then the Director of Public Prosecutions, said: "This trial has raised some fundamental questions about the treatment of victims and witnesses in the court process. Those questions require answers." I wonder if the questions have been answered; I once attended court in support of an innocent party, and I found the atmosphere of the court to be very intimidating.

'Sheltering behind legalese is a cop-out'

Chris Blackhurst is a former editor of *The Independent*. In his newspaper column he raged against BT's response to investor backlash over the £2.3m golden goodbye to its departing CEO.

Blackhurst wrote how BT, a multi-billion-pound global firm with the word 'communications' an actual part of its name, promised to overhaul its pay policies with the words: '...a broader range of performance factors and wider circumstances...a more structured process to help it step through the application of its discretion in the future.'

He continued that, instead of admitting that it had lost its way, 'BT attempted to soothe and gloss over the investor backlash with words straight out of the lawyers' lexicon *(upper left)* of safe twaddle'. He suggested that BT was: '...an organisation that is hidebound, stricken with fear, unable to proceed without a high degree of caution, incapable of saying "We screwed up, and we're sorry."'

'Running to lawyers, sheltering behind legalese, is a default, a cop-out,' Blackhurst continued. 'It is not the answer. Too often I have seen lawyers rule the roost. On a separate product safety issue, where fatalities had ensued, they were reluctant to let the management meet the relatives and express their condolences, because this could lead to an admission of liability.' Another example of *upper left* analytical thinking diagonally opposing *lower right* relational thinking.

Finally, Blackhurst made a plea: 'Please BT, in future, before you press 'send', stand back, and read what you are about to convey. Listen to the lawyers but remember, you're human and you're talking to humans.' Here, Blackhurst was stating that it is possible to convey analytical thinking in a relational way. Cognitive diversity calls it situational thinking.

Grenfell Tower fire: judge accused of 'disrespect'

In Chapter 11 we examined why male reporters of the Grenfell fire were called 'emotional retards'. Here, we examine why a retired judge was accused of 'disrespect'. The Grenfell Tower fire inquiry began on 14 September 2017 to investigate the causes of the fire and other related issues. The chairman of the inquiry was a retired judge.

Grenfell Tower was populated by poorer, mainly ethnic-minority residents. When the chairman concluded his short opening statement, barrister Michael Mansfield KC stood up to make a 'request' for the chairman to meet the survivors. I understand that a 'request' is not part of the inquisitorial procedure but is a way for the judge to meet the innocent parties who are otherwise not called upon in the inquiry process.

It was reported that the chairman angered survivors and relatives of those who died by 'refusing to acknowledge the request, turning his back on the survivors and leaving the room.'

Mr. Mansfield KC said that the chairman's refusal to listen to the survivors was 'disrespectful'. Melanie Phelan, a local community activist, agreed and added: "They don't seem to be very empathetic or even listening. We wanted him to listen to the survivors." In other words, the survivors wanted the chairman to exercise some relational thinking.

Some survivors left before the chairman had finished his opening statement, angered when he said he would not include residents on the inquiry assessment team because it would affect the inquiry's independence. Emma Dent Coad, the local MP, said "...the inquiry into the tragedy would not provide a full answer to those affected."

In terms of Cognitive Diversity At Work™, this is a classic example of an *upper left* analytical thinker (a retired judge) coming across to the survivors as gravely lacking in *lower right* relational thinking. He was reported to be disrespectful, lacking in empathy and listening skills, and insulting the residents (denying *lower mode instinctive* thinking) by claiming they would taint the intellectual independence (*upper mode* intellectual thinking) of the inquiry.

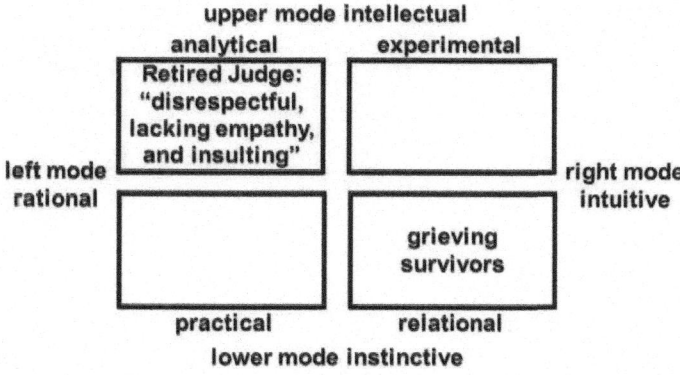

**How the grieving survivors viewed
the chairman of the Grenfell Inquiry**

Some *upper left* analytical, logical, and factual thinkers such as lawyers would benefit from cognitive diversity training to think situationally when dealing with grieving, innocent parties in court.

Chapter 14: Cognitive Diversity in Health

Photo by National Cancer Institute on Unsplash

Growing a bedside manner

Doctors have been told to watch more films, read more books, go to the theatre, and attend more concerts to improve their bedside manner. It looks like the doctor pictured above already enjoys those pastimes to the full: I certainly do so.

The recommendation came in the wake of a study, published in the *Journal of General Internal Medicine,* which revealed that medical students who devoted more time to the humanities are significantly better at empathising (*lower right* relational) with their patients. Such students also show higher tolerance of ambiguity, wisdom and emotional intelligence while also reporting lower levels of burnout.

The study stated that: 'Wisdom might very well be the single trait that encompasses of all of those other traits that define a well-rounded doctor: empathy, openness to possibilities, emotional resilience, mindfulness, humility, altruism, a knack for learning from life, plus a cathartic sense of humour. Yet, wisdom (*right mode* intuitive) is not a focus of today's medical education, which concentrates primarily on information and knowledge (*upper left* analytical).'

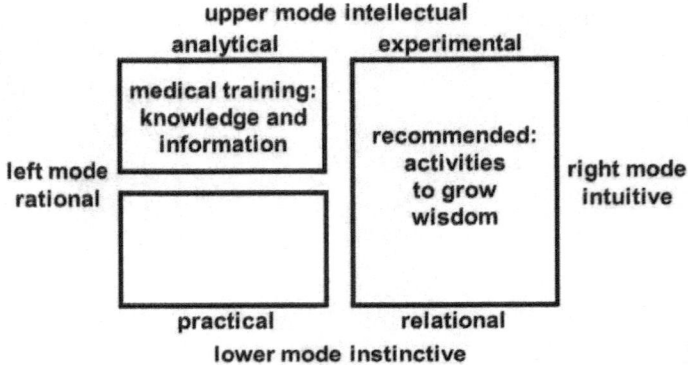

upper mode intellectual

analytical	experimental
medical training: knowledge and information	recommended: activities to grow wisdom

left mode rational ... **right mode intuitive**

| practical | relational |

lower mode instinctive

'Wisdom is not a focus of today's medical education'

Professor Marc Kahn of Tulane University said: "The humanities have often been pushed to the side in medical school curricula, but our data suggests that exposure to the arts is linked to important personal qualities for future physicians."

This is the first study to show this type of correlation, and the recommendation encompasses *right mode* intuitive thinking activities with a focus on *lower right* relational thinking. This would naturally result in an improvement in bedside manner.

Harmful arrogance in the operating theatre

A group of leading Scottish doctors have said that arrogant surgeons who bully patients and staff should attend 'ego classes' or be banned from the operating table. Simon Paterson-Brown, former chairman of the patient safety board at the Royal College of Surgeons of Edinburgh (RCSE), said his research in this area revealed that surgeons who attracted higher numbers of complaints from patients and staff tended to have more complications on the operating table.

He added: "There are surgeons who have poor leadership skills and who bully and harass other staff. It happens in Scotland, as it does in every other country."

Mr. Paterson-Brown was backed up by other influential medics including George Youngson (emeritus professor of paediatric surgery at Aberdeen university), Craig McIlhenny (director of the faculty of surgical training at the RCSE), Rhona Flin (emeritus professor), Nikki Maran (consultant anaesthetist at Edinburgh Royal Infirmary), and Steve Yule (an associate professor at Harvard university).

In their joint letter to the *British Medical Journal,* the doctors stated: 'The effects of surgical egos and poor behaviour on teamwork, clinical performance, and patient outcomes have been recognised for some time but are often poorly understood and very poorly managed.'

Cognitive Diversity At Work™ is not about personality testing; it is about thinking and thinking leads to behaviour. That arrogant and bullying behaviour can adversely affect patient outcomes is serious, and the thinking that precedes it is worthy of examination. As we know, analytical thinkers can appear as arrogant to relational thinkers such as nursing staff, and especially to patients who are feeling vulnerable.

The leading Scottish doctors, cited above, believe surgeons should attend courses to hone non-technical skills such as decision-making, communication *(lower right)*, leadership *(upper right)* and 'situation awareness'. Coincidentally, a practical workshop addressing communication is offered at cognitivediversity.co.uk/workshops.

What Mr. Paterson-Brown calls situation awareness, cognitive diversity calls situational behaviour. NLP teaches that thinking precedes behaviour. Hence, if you want to adjust your behaviour, you first adjust your thinking. When you think situationally, you can adjust your thinking and behaviour to the other people in the situation. This is not easy to do, it may even feel counter-intuitive and needs to be practised time and time again until it becomes second nature. I should know...

'Ten-minute appointments are unfit for purpose'

It was reported in May 2019 that the NHS was seeing the first sustained fall in GP numbers in the UK for 50 years. An analysis by the Nuffield Trust think tank showed the number of GPs per 100,000 patients had fallen from nearly 65 in 2014 to 60 in 2018. Patient groups said the fall was causing real difficulties in making appointments.

One of the fallouts of this situation is the ten-minute limit on appointments and only one health condition per appointment. There are clearly many factors at work here, because I recall having no difficulty getting appointments in the 1960s, when records show that the number of GPs per 100,000 patients could be as low as 42.

In those days GPs worked from home, and one simply walked in and waited to be seen. One did not have to telephone to make an appointment: in any case, few people had a telephone at home. The receptionist was usually the doctor's wife in what was in reality a small family firm. I cannot recall the duration of appointments, but they never seemed rushed. You put your medical card through a hatch and waited to be called. Everybody watched everybody else like a hawk to make sure that nobody jumped the queue!

In May 2019, the Royal College of General Practitioners (RCGP) reported that the current system of doctors' appointments was unfit for purpose. The report recommended that consultations should last at least 15 minutes instead of the standard ten minutes.

Records show that the average GP consultation in the UK lasts 9.2 minutes, which is one of the lowest among economically advanced nations. My own local GP practice tells patients to present with only one problem in a ten-minute consultation.

The then chair of the RCGP, Professor Helen Stokes-Lampard, said that it was increasingly rare for a patient to present with just a single health condition and doctors cannot deal with more than one condition in only ten minutes. "GPs want to deliver truly holistic *(upper right)* care to patients considering all the physical, social, and psychological factors impacting on their health. But that depends on doctors spending more time with patients, with the necessary resources and people to ensure that happens."

So, it seems that the ideal situation is one of GPs (*upper left* technical) practising with empathy and great communications skills (*lower right* relational) having the 'necessary resources and people to ensure that happens' (*lower left* practical).

I wonder if the *lower left* practical support is lacking in some way, resulting in GPs' workload soaring, GP numbers falling, thereby creating a vicious spiral? Are there sufficient supporting resources? If there are, is NHS bureaucracy *(lower left)* getting in the way?

District nurses becoming 'task-focused'

A study by the Royal College of Nursing (RCN) and the Queen's Nursing Institute found that district nursing – which provides care in people's homes and nursing homes – was significantly under-resourced. Our neighbour opposite is a retired District Nurse and as a volunteer still sets a wonderful example in caring for people in the village, even though her mobility is much impaired.

The number of full-time equivalent district nurses working in the NHS in England fell from 7,055 in 2009 to 4,031 in 2019, a drop of 43%. This results in a ratio of one District Nurse for every 14,000 people.

The study reported that, as a result, district nurses were becoming 'task-focused' and called for increased investment. When I was trained in leadership by the Royal Air Force, I was taught to balance task needs, team needs, and individual needs. If one need is prioritised, it will be at the expense of at least one of the other two.

I can imagine that if district nurses are 'task-focused' *(lower left)* then patients' individual needs *(lower right)* could suffer.

Why do some women quit surgical training?

The question has been posed in the national press: 'Why are there so few women surgeons in the UK?' This subchapter looks at reasons why some women leave surgical training, and why some trained women surgeons leave the profession.

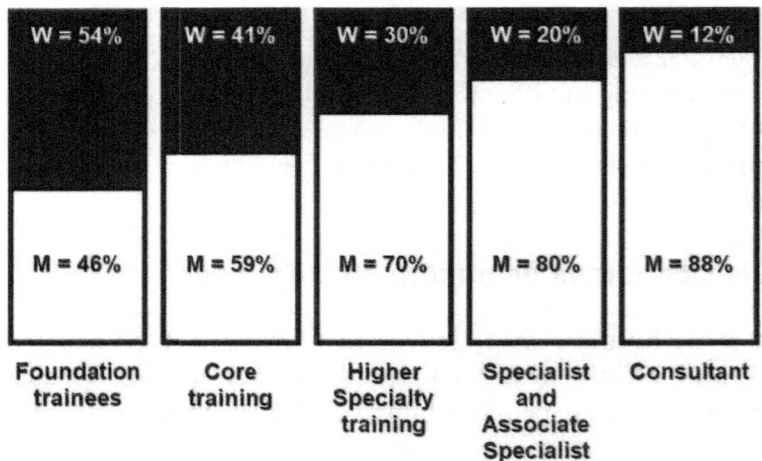

Surgeons, men and women, in England in 2018

In 2018 the *British Medical Journal (BMJ)* stated '...while 54% of foundation trainees in surgery are women...12% of consultant surgeons are women.' (14). The message is clear: plenty of women start surgical careers, but many leave surgery; some even leave the NHS.

Some women leave during surgical training and never qualify as surgeons. A female junior doctor who left surgical training was quoted as saying that she had been '…hurled into a world of egomaniac men. Every day, every minute, you have to dress like a man, think like a man, talk like a man.'

She described surgery as having a masculine, macho culture. This description will not be analysed here, because the concepts of masculinity and femininity are outside the scope of this book.

She did not quit because of the so-called macho culture. She quit because she found the demands of the surgical training made it impossible for her to care for her infant son.

Cognitive Diversity At Work™ offers the following insights.

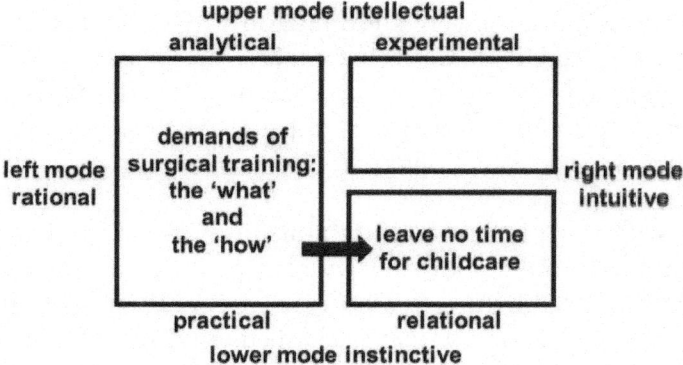

The demands of surgical training can make childcare "impossible"

Surgical skills are transferred person-to-person, which requires *lower right relational* thinking. However, the sheer volume of material content in terms of the 'what' and the 'how' combine to impose rational *left mode* demands that can overwhelm some trainees.

If a job is tough, then the training is meant to be tough and leave the trainee in no doubt about the challenges they will face on the job. Only those who pass the training can be expected to cope on the job. As a General once said: "Train hard, fight easy". However, the intensive training seems to leave some junior doctors with no time for family, and they choose to leave surgery.

I hope that they move on to other specialisations within the NHS such as General Practice, paediatrics, psychiatry, clinical oncology, and dentistry. This may in fact be so, since NHS Digital has reported that every specialty group across hospital and community health services has seen an increase in the proportion of women.

Why do some trained female surgeons quit?

It is reported that the working life of surgeons can be highly pressured, unpredictable, and brutally punishing. I witnessed this myself at St Vincent's Hospital in Melbourne, Australia. My wife tripped in Carlton Gardens, broke her wrist, and was prepped for surgery at noon the next day. Next day, the surgical team had been operating since early morning, and then a casualty was admitted at noon.

My wife was put on hold without food or water whilst the team spent the rest of the day saving the casualty's hands. Then after midnight they performed a beautiful repair on my wife's wrist. I found their achievements quite humbling, deeply moving, and worthy of the highest respect. Their work is certainly tough.

What could make it even tougher? There is evidence that systemic bureaucracy in the NHS gets in the way and prevents frontline medics, such as surgeons, doing their jobs how they were trained to do them. As a result, surgeons can arrive home late, worn down, frustrated, and exhausted.

Under these conditions, some women believe that it is not possible to be both a good surgeon and a good mother. Some quit the NHS to be a good mother.

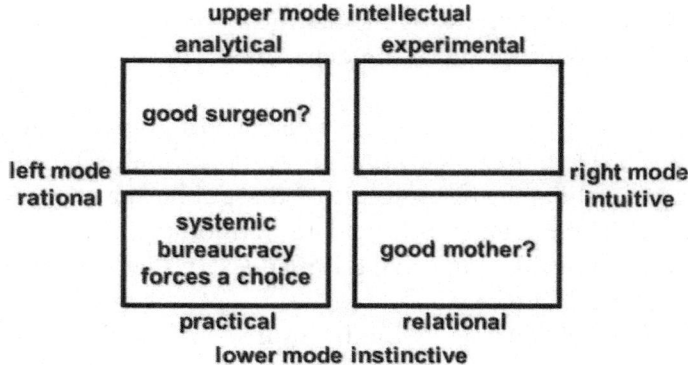

upper mode intellectual
analytical   experimental

good surgeon?

left mode   **right mode**
rational   **intuitive**

systemic bureaucracy forces a choice   good mother?

practical   relational
lower mode instinctive

A devastating impact of bureaucracy in the NHS

Surgeons require very strong *upper left* analytical thinking in terms of what to do, and very strong *lower left* practical thinking in how to do that. They rely on the *lower left* management to provide all the supporting resources.

Surgeons and management can be mutually supportive and sympathetic and can quickly cotton on to each other's thinking. However, this speed of communication can lead to shorthand, assumptions, and hence false understandings. With full support, and a minimum of bureaucracy, I can imagine surgeons who are mothers could have sufficient time and energy for caring for their children and be totally fulfilled as human beings.

When NHS bureaucracy imposes an additional and unnecessary burden on top of an already tough job there is evidence that it prevents proper exercise of strong *lower right* relational thinking. Since very significantly more women than men have strong relational thinking preferences, this disproportionally affects women. One outcome of this is the inability to care for their children, a symptom of which is intolerable stress which is not sustainable – hence, some mothers quit surgery.

On a happier note, some women do get to the top in surgery. The surgeon who saved my brother-in-law's life with a quadruple heart bypass at St George's Tooting is a female professor and also head of the department: bravo!

Cognitive Diversity At Work™ believes that a solution lies in curbing NHS bureaucracy. As Dr Abraham Sukumar wrote on *Quora:* 'It is in the interest of the public that they give doctors the leadership role and responsibility in all matters concerning health…and make it mandatory that members of the medical profession are heads of hospitals.' This organisational change would ensure that administration comes under the control of doctors, and not vice versa.

On a resettlement course I ran for senior officers retiring from the armed forces, a Major General said to me: "Change tack, Michael, and join the NHS!" When I protested that I knew nothing about the NHS, he laughed: "That's the whole point!" When I relayed this story to a chum, a senior manager in the NHS, he told me that I would not like working in the NHS, because it is so political. Now I understand that half of all staff in the NHS are bureaucrats - managers and administrators - with no medical qualifications.

Of course, removing bureaucracy by itself will not cure all the ills of the NHS. The NHS business model is by common consent 'broken'. Satirists joke that the UK economy is fast becoming the NHS with a country attached. I recommend that a new business model is constructed by a committee employing cognitive diversity thinking in all four quadrants. The Terms of Reference would include the eradication of bureaucracy and learning from best practice in other countries. Bureaucracy is a very heavy and cosy comfort blanket.

A surgeon's tale: analyse first, reflect later

"Focusing on facts and analysis can look like arrogance", an eminent surgeon told his interviewer. "It's a very fine line you walk between confidence in yourself and arrogance, and some people tip over onto the arrogant side. It's self-protection, though. Once you start doubting yourself, it is time to stop. A couple of deaths (on the operating table) can destroy you psychologically."

The strain of being a parent and a surgeon is not restricted to women. He was painfully aware of being an absent father to his own children. Yet there were very few surgeons doing what he did, and he felt a strong emotional connection *(lower right)* with his patients.

Here we see how surgeons focusing on *upper left* facts and analysis can appear to be arrogant, when they are not meaning to be. They are in reality choosing detachment from their *lower right* emotional response in real-time life and death situations. He learned his trade the hard way, dealing with victims during the height of the Troubles in Northern Ireland.

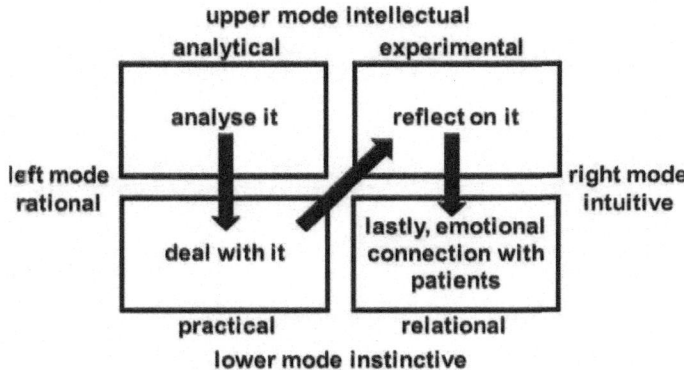

How surgeons deal with a difficult situation

Amongst the trauma he realised that the reactions of the best surgeons were always the same. "Faced with a difficult situation, you analyse it *(upper left)* and deal with it *(lower left)*, then reflect on it *(upper right)* later." After reflection, he was able to deal with the worries and concerns of his patients and their relatives.

Chapter 15: Cognitive Diversity in Education

Photo by Adam Winger on Unsplash

Potential shortage of teachers in England

There are many issues to be covered in Education. In this book I will limit myself to exploring one issue: the reported potential shortage of teachers in the state sector in England (15).

As of November 2018, the total full-time equivalent (FTE) number of teachers in state schools in England was 453,000. The vacancy rate at the end of 2018 was less than 0.5%. I would not call that a significant shortage. So how was there a potential shortage looming, and what could exacerbate the problem?

In recent years, the overall number of teachers did not keep pace with increasing pupil numbers, and the ratio of pupils to qualified teachers increased from 17.8 in 2011 to 18.9 in 2018. Pupil numbers were expected to continue rising, driven by a projected 15% increase in the number of secondary school pupils between 2018 and 2024. This, along with other factors such as the ambition for more pupils to take the English Baccalaureate combination of GCSE subjects, meant that pressure on teacher recruitment could increase further.

In summary, there did seem to be a potential shortage of teachers in England. Let us explore what Cognitive Diversity At Work™ has to say regarding the recruitment and retention of teachers in England.

Teaching is a vocation

The art of teaching, regardless of the subject matter being taught, relies on strong thinking preferences in relational thinking. So strong that teaching is one of those careers regarded as a vocation – a way of life. It requires dedication.

I saw this at first hand in my cousin Barbara: 16 years older than me, she was Head Girl at Bradford Girls' Grammar School and was expected to go up to Oxford University. Instead, she went straight into teacher training.

She dedicated her life to teaching and became a Head of a large Comprehensive school. She retired early on health grounds, burned out, and died much too young. Barbara was my mentor; I still miss her special friendship and good counsel.

Newly qualified teachers drop out

Department for Education (DfE) data shows that the number who completed their teacher training but never entered the classroom tripled in six years – from 3,600 in 2006 to 10,800 in 2011. The cost to the taxpayer of training them was estimated to be just under £1bn. The *Teacher Recruitment and Retention Strategy* of 28 January 2019 stated that 'the process to become a teacher is too complicated and burdensome.'

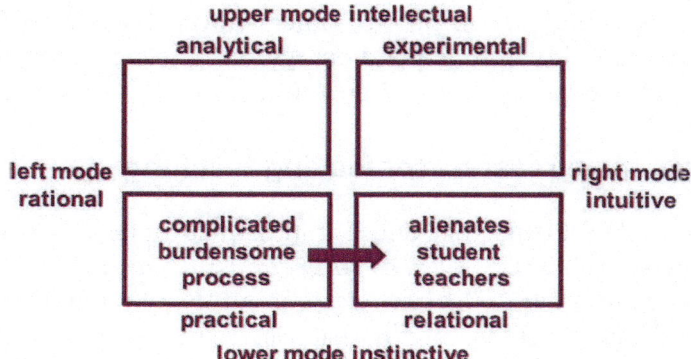

Teacher training process puts some students off teaching

Processes sit in the *lower left* thinking quadrant, and maybe groupthink set in. In other words, trainees were driven to expend energy on process and procedures *(lower left)* at the expense of learning how to teach *(lower right)*.

Experienced teachers drop out

The DfE report *School Workforce in England* of November 2018 stated that 22.5% of newly qualified entrants to the sector in 2016 were not recorded as working in the state sector in 2018. The five year out-of-service-rate for 2013 entrants was 32.3%. The ten year out-of-service rate for 2009 entrants was 38% and had been between 34.4% and 40.3% in each year since 1997. So, about four out of ten experienced teachers dropped out by their tenth year.

Dr Mary Bousted, when general secretary of the Association of Teachers and Lecturers (ATL), told a conference that newly qualified teachers "...learn as they work with exhausted and stressed colleagues that teaching has become a profession which is incompatible with a normal life.

"Too many school leaders, driven by fear of inspection, drive their teaching staff to do things which add not one jot to the quality of teaching but to bureaucratic work, filling forms, inputting data and using three different coloured pens for 'deep marking' and so on." In other words, newly qualified teachers are driven to expend energy on bureaucracy *(lower left)* at the expense of teaching *(lower right)*.

Three main reasons for leaving teaching

In October 2014, the Office for Standards in Education (Ofsted) published *Ofsted Inspections: Clarifications for Schools,* in order to "confirm facts about the requirements of Ofsted and to dispel myths that can result in unnecessary workloads in schools."

Yet in September 2017 the Department for Education surveyed ex-teachers and published a report showing that workload, government policy and lack of support from leadership were cited as the three main reasons for leaving teaching. Recent governments have noted workload as 'the most frequently cited reason for teachers wanting to leave the profession' and have stated that it 'is too high and must be reduced.'

In 2018, *The Teaching & Learning International Survey* reported that 53% of primary teachers and 57% of lower-secondary school teachers felt that their workload was unmanageable.

In 2019, *The Teacher Workload Survey* reported that teachers worked an average of 49.5 hours a week, of which 21.3 hours were spent teaching. There was anecdotal evidence of 60 to 70-hour weeks. Most respondents to the survey reported that they could not complete their workload within their contracted hours, that they did not have an acceptable workload, and that they did not achieve a good work-life balance.

In January 2019, *The Teacher Recruitment and Retention Strategy* was published. Dr Mary Bousted, then the Joint General Secretary of the National Education Union (NEU) stated: "The strategy will not be a game-changer for the major problems of excessive and unnecessary workload.. "

Dr Bousted has also said: "The reasons that so many leave the profession so quickly are not a mystery to us. When faced with impossible workloads, endless accountability, a testing culture run riot, and flat or underfunded pay deals year after year, it is all too common for good teachers to leave the profession."

In March 2019, with regard to teacher workload and wellbeing, the DfE announced that a new advisory group had been set up to 'look at how teachers and school leaders can be better supported to deal with the pressures of the job.' Does this mean that the DfE believed the pressures could not be reduced, and the best the DfE could offer was 'support'?

Mark Baker, when president of the ATL, said that "...teachers faced so much bureaucracy driven by mistrust, driven by an unquenchable thirst for data but so utterly pointless". This even included asking teachers to take photographs of practical lessons to prove that they had taken place. In other words, experienced teachers are driven to expend energy on bureaucracy *(lower left)* at the expense of teaching *(lower right)*.

Anecdotal evidence of bureaucracy

I define bureaucracy in education as the indirect, non-value adding administrative burden imposed on teachers by the Department for Education and local authorities.

An English teacher was reported as quitting her secondary school 'to get her life back'. She estimated that she was working a 60 to 70-hour week, six days a week, at school and at home. She said her job was incompatible with "the right work-life balance" and helping her children: "I've realised that I don't have the time to be a good family member." This perhaps echoes the reasons given by women choosing to be either 'good mothers' or 'good surgeons'.

After five years in the teaching profession, she had spoken to newly qualified teachers who were ready to quit much earlier than that. She said of the young teachers – men and women – who were deciding against the career: "These are all passionate and incredibly talented people. It's such a shame." I would call it a tragic waste of special talent.

I was a school governor at my sons' schools in the 1980s and I found the governor's workload acceptable. However, when I volunteered as a governor in the 2010s, I was immediately appalled at the high level of bureaucracy and the thud of paperwork hitting my door mat.

I was especially concerned at the weight of documentation for an Ofsted inspection. When the DfE announced that the huge report was no longer necessary, I was dismayed when the Head Teacher decided to continue completing it.

The ethos and the teaching at the school were both excellent. The pupils were a delight to talk to and mature beyond their years. I concluded that a 'Satisfactory' grade could easily be attained by focusing on teaching alone. Yet a grading as 'Satisfactory' year after year was derided by the authorities as 'coasting': to be graded 'Outstanding' became the goal.

However, it became clear to me that to achieve an 'Outstanding' grade, parents, staff, and governors would have to be totally committed to non-value adding extracurricular activities to turn the school into some sort of beacon of social engineering in the local community.

I resigned. With a very strong preference for *upper right* quadrant strategic thinking, I am totally turned off by the diagonally opposite *lower left* quadrant bureaucratic thinking. Very interestingly, the current Head Teacher was a practising barrister *(upper left analytical)* who saw the light and retrained as a teacher *(lower right relational)*.

Bureaucracy versus teaching

Lower left quadrant bureaucrats and *lower right* quadrant teachers can be in synergy, but the difference in working styles can be challenging. The ideal scenario would be the minimum of rational *left mode* bureaucracy enabling intuitive *right mode* teachers to maximise value adding teaching with the lightest possible reporting burden.

Bureaucrats think strongly in terms of policy, protocols, process, procedure, planning, resourcing, scheduling, detailed data, monitoring, controlling, budgets, cost planning, actual spend, forecasting of costs to completion, hierarchies of control, risk aversion, and so on.

Teachers think strongly in terms of personal interaction, creativity, sensing feedback, sensing understanding, inspiring and motivating students, setting a personal example, communicating, projecting themselves and so on. Detailed bureaucracy is anathema to these thinkers.

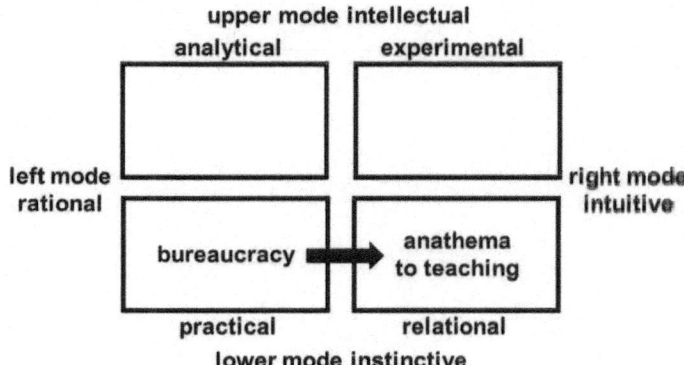

The thinking preferences of teachers and bureaucrats are quite different. So why are teachers spending so much of their time on bureaucracy? Cognitive Diversity At Work™ recommends that educational management reduces bureaucracy to a minimum thereby liberating teachers to focus on teaching. The same can be said for liberating front-line staff in the NHS, as well as in other branches of the public sector.

Chapter 16: Women in STEM

'Girls don't like physics'

'Girls don't like physics as they won't do the hard maths', a report by Joe Pinkstone, Science Correspondent of *The Telegraph,* set me thinking. He was quoting Katharine Birbalsingh, headteacher of the Michaela School, talking about her girls taking A levels. Michaela Community School is an 11–18 mixed boys and girls, free secondary school and sixth form in Wembley, London.

Suella Braverman KC MP, twice Home Secretary, was the first chair of governors. It has been described as the 'strictest school in Britain'. In both 2022 and 2023 the value-added (progress) score at GCSE level was the highest for any school in England.

As reported by Joe Pinkstone, a simple statement of fact by headteacher Katharine Birbalsingh erupted into two major rows. She was briefing the House of Commons science and technology committee about her sixth-form A level classes comprising boys and girls. She told MPs that girls comprise the majority of students in her biology, chemistry, and maths classes, but only 16% in physics.

The chairman of the committee asked why girls were a minority in physics. Birbalsingh replied: "I just think they don't like it. There is a lot of hard maths in there that I think they would rather not do." Cue a major row about female stereotypes in A level physics, with MPs, scientists, teachers, and others all furiously condemning her remarks.

For example, Rachel Youngman, Deputy Chief Executive of the Institute of Physics (IOP) said: "The IOP is very concerned at the continued use of outdated stereotypes, as we firmly believe physics is for everyone regardless of their background or gender. Outdated ideas need to be eradicated; all young people need to be encouraged to learn physics."

Jim Al-Khalili, academic and broadcaster, Professor of Theoretical Physics at the University of Surrey, called Birbalsingh's remarks "...utter, awful nonsense...regressive tripe".

Did Birbalsingh use stereotypes? For example, when she said that girls don't like physics, did she mean 'all girls don't like physics', or 'physics is not for girls' or 'girls can't do physics'? And when she said that girls would rather not do hard maths, did she mean 'all girls would rather not do hard maths' or 'hard maths is not for girls' or 'girls can't do hard maths'?

I believe that Birbalsingh did not use such stereotypes, that her words were factual, taken out of context, and she did not use 'outdated stereotypes' as Youngman believed.

The STEM pipeline

It set me thinking about the STEM pipeline, from girls studying STEM A levels at school to the number of women working in STEM. I quickly discovered that many influential people think that there are not enough women in STEM.

People such as Brian Cox, TV presenter and professor of particle physics, who has said: "The problem is, we don't have enough women going into certain areas, particularly engineering."

Riad Mannan wrote in *New Engineer* in March 2021: 'For many years, around the world, it has been recognised that there is a skills shortage in engineering.' This implies that there aren't enough men going into engineering, either. Mannan also noted that women comprise some 13% of UK engineers; could a shortfall be made up by women?

All of the above poses some interesting questions. What is STEM? What are the STEM A levels? How many girls take STEM A levels? Are there gender stereotypes in STEM A levels? Are there gender stereotypes in any A level subjects?

How many women work in STEM? Do we need more women in STEM? Can teachers inspire more girls into STEM? Can teachers inspire girls into STEM trades? If teachers can't, who can inspire girls into STEM?

Are some women who could work in STEM choosing to work outside STEM, and if so, why? Cognitive Diversity at Work™ answers these questions, starting with 'What is STEM?'

So, what is STEM?

STEM stands for science, technology, engineering, and mathematics. Let's explore each in turn.

Science is knowledge, stored in our brains with useful back up in physical storage such as books. Scientific knowledge is usually created in laboratories through research, observation, setting hypotheses, experimentation, and testing. Science in UK schools is compulsory to GCSE level – to Year 11 - and comprises biology, chemistry, and physics:-

- Biology for our knowledge of life in all its forms. Its themes include the hereditary process through genes and evolution, and energy processing allowing organisms to move, grow, and reproduce. Individual organisms die, but life carries on through reproduction.

- Chemistry for our knowledge of all the 118 known elements that make up matter. Chemistry explains their composition, structure, properties, behaviour, and the changes they undergo when reacting with other elements or combinations of elements.

- Physics for the knowledge of matter in motion through space and time, from sub-atomic particles to whole galaxies, and the related entities of mass, momentum, kinetic energy, potential energy, force, acceleration, work, power, heat, light, and sound.

Technology is the physical application of scientific knowledge for making things in the real world. It takes inputs and produces outputs. Technology can be hardware or software, or a mix. Technology also includes the knowledge, training, skills, competency, experience, and procedures in how to use it.

Sometimes it's difficult to know where technology starts and ends. Everywhere you look, the modern world depends on many interconnected technologies. Technologies beget technologies that beget technologies and so on. For example, mobile phone technology relies on many technologies, including microchip technology.

Microchips are themselves the products of many technologies. The most advanced microchips are made by machines using EUV (extreme ultraviolet) lithography technology. The $200m machines are made by only one company in the world: ASML (Advanced Semiconductor Materials Lithography) in Holland.

Chris Miller, assistant professor at the Fletcher School at Tufts University, has called the ASML machines "...among the most complicated devices ever made." The machines are strategically important, and China is not allowed to buy them.

The machines neatly illustrate the interdependence between many technologies. Mobile phone manufacturers who are short of microchips demand more microchips from microchip manufacturers, who demand more microchip-making machines from ASML, who then need more components from their suppliers, who then struggle to meet ASML's demand because of their own shortage of microchips: Catch-22!

Engineering has been around for thousands of years. Many ancient structures such as the Colosseum and Parthenon in Rome are still standing after nearly 2000 years. They were engineered using 'rule of thumb' methods before scientific knowledge and technology were developed. Modern engineering can now make use of scientific knowledge, new technologies, computing, and advanced maths.

Literally everything you use has been engineered into existence. The modern world owes its existence to engineers. Engineering can be unappreciated and undervalued in the UK.

Mathematics is the global lingua franca of science, technology, and engineering. Numbers are not a matter of subjective opinion and interpretation in the way that words can be. They are objectively either right or wrong. I should know. My degree in aeronautical engineering was wall-to-wall hard maths.

To sum up STEM, let's use your mobile phone as an example. Your mobile phone was designed by engineers, each specialising in a science-based technology such as integrated circuits, software, wi-fi, Bluetooth, digital communications, the internet, aerials, liquid crystal displays, touchscreens, microphones, speakers, batteries, cameras, optics and so on.

The chief engineer orchestrated the hardware and software engineers to design a phone that appealed to you in terms of price, functionality, performance, capacity, ease of use, battery life, appearance, size, weight, durability, maintainability, repairability, product support, and maybe eco-friendly disposal. Your phone is just one of many elements in a world-wide communications system.

In the palm of your hand, you have functionality that in the 1980s would have filled an entire floor of an office building. This incredible miniaturisation is down to science, technology, engineering, and mathematics: STEM!

Having gained an understanding of STEM, we can now explore the academic subjects that underpin it. What are the STEM A levels, and how many girls take them?

How many girls take STEM A levels?

The UK Department for Education define six A level subjects for careers in STEM. They are computing, physics, further maths, maths, chemistry, and biology. On average each STEM candidate takes just two STEM subjects. I took three: maths, further maths, and physics.

The table opposite shows the STEM A level candidates in England in 2022. The source is Ofqual (16):

STEM A levels as defined by DfE	Boys who took the A level	Girls who took the A level	Total who took the A level	Boys as % of total who took the A level	Girls as % of total who took the A level
	B	G	B+G	B÷(B+G)	G÷(B+G)
Computing	12565	2245	14810	85%	15%
Physics	27945	8345	36290	77%	23%
Fr Maths	10260	4025	14285	72%	28%
Maths	55250	33065	88315	63%	37%
Chemistry	24110	30030	54140	45%	55%
Biology	23740	41525	65265	36%	64%

STEM A level candidates in England in 2022

Ofqual use the name computing whereas Department for Education (DfE) use the name computer science. Since I am using Ofqual statistics I will use the name computing.

At the national level, girls comprised 23% of all students who sat physics. Hence, it was normal for Birbalsingh's girls to be in the minority in her school's physics class. From the table above we can see that boys comprised the majority of students who sat physics, and girls comprised the majority of students who sat biology.

Does this infer stereotypes such as 'physics is for boys', and 'biology is for girls'? For an answer we need to look at the bigger picture.

DfE show that a total of 156,137 girls and 128,240 boys sat A levels in England in 2022 (17). The table overleaf shows the real popularity of A level STEM subjects in England in 2022:

STEM A levels as defined by DfE	Boys who took the A level	Girls who took the A level	Boys as % of all boys who sat A levels (popularity with all boys) B÷	Girls as % of all girls who sat A levels (popularity with all girls) G÷
	B	G	128,240	156,137
Computing	12565	2245	10%	1%
Fr Maths	10260	4025	8%	3%
Physics	27945	8345	22%	5%
Chemistry	24110	30030	19%	19%
Maths	55250	33065	43%	21%
Biology	23740	41525	19%	27%

**Popularity of STEM subjects
with all A level candidates in England in 2022**

As you can see, physics was unpopular with 78% of all boys, and 95% of all girls. A level physics is therefore 'not for everyone' as Rachel Youngman claimed. Only biology was more popular among girls than boys. The most popular STEM subject of all was maths yet 57% of all boys avoided it.

Some look for reasons why further maths, maths, computing, and physics are more popular with boys than girls. Most explain it in terms of identity diversity such as 'they are male subjects'. Cognitive diversity offers a different explanation, with new insights and a fresh perspective in terms of 'how you think' rather than 'what you are'.

First, let us look at the thinking preferences associated with further maths and maths. The basis for further maths and maths is strong or very strong analytical thinking, which is logical, fact-based, and quantitative. Although by no means all men have this preference, there are significantly more men than women who do:

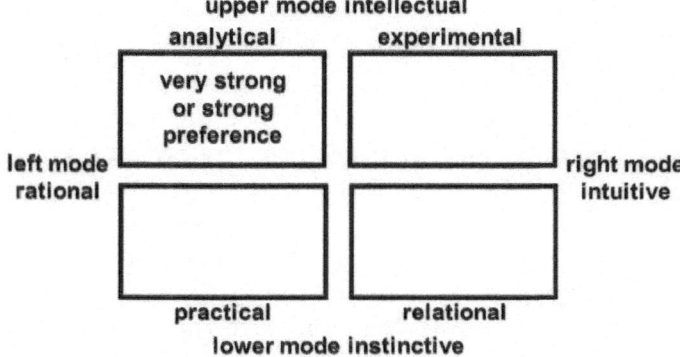

**Significantly more men than women
have this profile for further maths and maths**

Let us now look at the sciences of physics and computing. This is when analytical thinking is joined by experimental thinking.

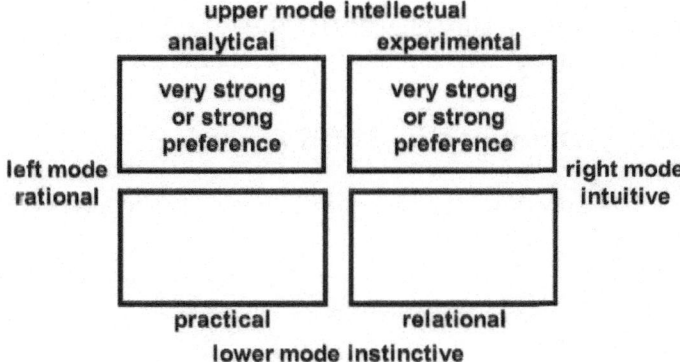

**Significantly more men than women
have this profile for physics and computing**

Thus, by extrapolating back from men and women at work to boys and girls at school, Cognitive Diversity At Work™ explains why we find significantly more boys than girls taking A levels in computing, physics, further maths, and maths. The table of popularity shows that most boys avoid these STEM subjects, because not all boys have a strong or very strong preference for analytical thinking.

What about Rachel Youngman's statement that 'physics is for everyone'? Well, in a way it is - up to Year 11 - since the National Curriculum mandates Science GCSE (comprising biology, chemistry, and physics) for every boy and girl, pass or fail.

What about Katharine Birbalsingh's comment about hard maths? I can personally attest to the difficulty of doing the hard maths. My honours degree in aeronautical engineering at Imperial College was only achieved by slogging through the wall-to-wall hard maths by sheer will power, hard grind, and stress. It did not come naturally. Maybe my love of aviation was stronger than my analytical thinking!

My final year tutorial group included the only student to obtain a First Class Honours out of our class of 20. Appreciating how sharp is a first-class analytical mind at first hand is a massive reality check! (By the way, I can't recall any girls in my final year.)

Gender stereotypes in STEM A levels?

The only stereotype in this story is 'physics is for everyone': since only 5% of all girls and 22% of all boys take physics at A level, there can be no business case for resourcing physics teaching at A level for everyone.

My conclusion is that Katharine Birbalsingh did not use stereotypes such as 'physics is not for girls' or 'hard maths is not for girls'. She stated the truth that at A level some girls do like physics and hard maths, but they are in the minority.

Cognitive Diversity At Work™ explains this by showing that some girls do have the strong thinking preferences to like physics and hard maths, but the majority do not. Boys and girls take STEM A levels. There are no gender stereotypes in STEM A levels in general, or maths and physics in particular.

Gender stereotypes in any A levels?

We have dealt with a row about gender stereotypes in maths and physics A levels. Are there gender stereotypes in any A level subjects? The DfE publishes the breakdown of candidates taking each A level subject in England in the following format (17). The percentages for each subject in 2022 were:

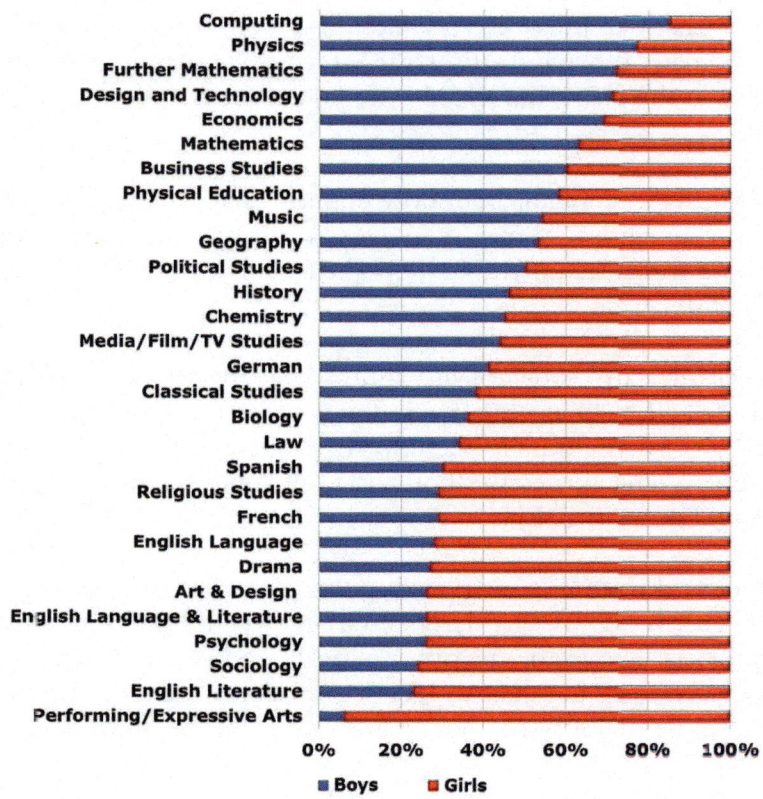

DfE: A level candidates in England 2022

For example, of the candidates who took computing, 85% were boys and 15% were girls. Cognitive Diversity At Work™ can think of four ways of presenting the data differently.

Firstly, it is not apparent that more girls than boys take A levels. 156,137 girls and 128,240 boys took A levels in England in 2022. All other things being equal, with 22% more girls than boys, one can expect their percentages to be inflated.

Secondly, since each subject sums up to 100% it is not apparent how many candidates actually took each subject. For example, music is very high in the chart but only 5,270 candidates (boys and girls) sat it. Conversely, sociology is very low in the chart, but 42,820 candidates (boys and girls) took it.

Thirdly, it is not apparent how popular each subject was with boys or girls. It may come as a surprise to learn that computing (2,245) was more popular with girls than German (1,560).

Fourthly, any subject with more than 50% boys is usually described as being 'male', and any subject with more than 50% girls is usually described as being 'female'. This stereotyping misses the point that all subjects are taken by both boys and girls.

Under this stereotyping, only political studies can appear to be 'balanced' or 'gender neutral' between boys and girls. Subjects above or below political studies are therefore deemed to be in a state of 'gender imbalance'. On this simple basis, the majority of subjects are deemed to be 'female'.

Computing is even described as being 'the most disproportionately male subject' and English literature is described as being 'the most disproportionately female subject'. These are subjective judgements, as if the natural state should be equal percentages of male and female in all subjects.

Over the years, commentators sum up the situation as a 'persistent gender imbalance in A level subjects' as if there is a national problem that needs to put right somehow, no doubt with massive public spending funded by borrowing. My preferred presentation is to show the popularity of each subject with boys and girls separately:

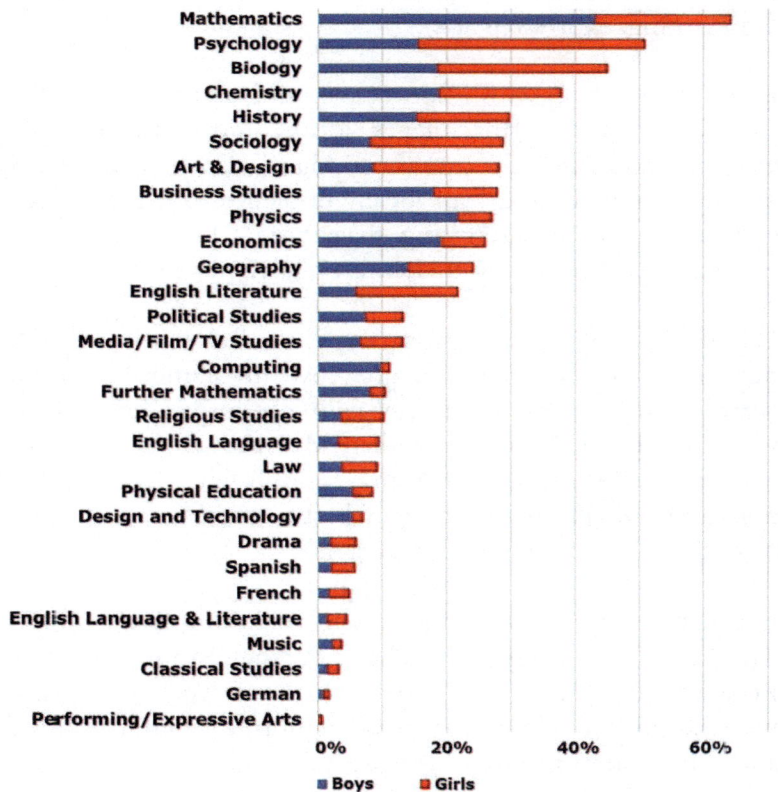

Popularity of A level subjects England 2022

I define the popularity of any subject with boys as:
(number of boys who took the subject) divided by
(total number of boys who took A levels) as a percentage,

and the popularity of any subject with girls as: (number of girls who took the subject) divided by (total number of girls who took A levels) as a percentage.

Hence the real popularity of computing with girls was only 1.4% and not 15% as in the DfE graph. This means that computing was not popular with 98.6% of all girls taking A levels in 2022. This popularity format does not lend itself to being 'gendered'. It is ranked from the most popular subject with all candidates (maths) to the least popular (performing/expressive arts).

It could even help with resource planning and budgeting for schools and sixth form colleges, locally and nationally. For example, one can see a case for foreign language teachers to be multi-lingual, or at least locally pooled in one sixth-form college. It is also interesting that three STEM subjects – mathematics, biology, and chemistry – are in the top four.

Having dealt with gender stereotypes in all A levels, we will now look at the second major row involving Katharine Birbalsingh. She was accused of failing to inspire her girls to work in STEM. Carol Monaghan MP (previously a physics teacher and Head of Science in a school) said: "… I prided myself on the number of my female students who went on to have highly successful STEM careers".

Her views were supported by others including Layla Moran MP (also once a physics teacher), Rachel Youngman, and Professor Al-Khalili. So, what are the facts? How many women work in STEM, do we need more women in STEM, and can teachers inspire more girls into STEM?

How many women work in STEM?

Nomis shows the number of women working in STEM in the UK in 2022 (18). In the UK in 2022 the total working population was 32,609,500 comprising 17,027,900 men and

15,531,600 women. The table below shows how many women and men were working in STEM in 2022:

STEM jobs	Women in the jobs	% of all working women	Men in the jobs	% of all working men
Directors				
Technology IT and Telecoms	29800	0.2%	147200	0.9%
Professionals				
Science: Natural and Social Sciences, R&D	152700	1.0%	174800	1.0%
Technology IT and Telecoms	245100	1.6%	1024400	6.0%
Engineering	65100	0.4%	403700	2.4%
Technicians				
Science	25000	0.2%	30300	0.2%
Technology	65900	0.4%	213800	1.2%
Engineering	77300	0.5%	251400	1.5%
Totals	660900	4.3%	2245600	13.2%

Women and men working in STEM in the UK in 2022

Nomis does not show maths occupations *per se*, but all STEM occupations are underpinned by maths. The figures show that STEM occupations are three times more popular with men than women: 13.2% to 4.3%.

Do we need more women in STEM?

In 2021, *STEM Learning* reported an estimated shortfall of over 173,000 workers in the UK STEM sector (19). Cognitive Diversity At Work™ would like to analyse the shortfall but at the time of writing, *STEM Learning* have not provided a demographic breakdown of the shortfall.

Any shortfall in STEM grieves me personally since I dedicated my first career to engineering and manufacturing in the aircraft, electronics, and software systems industries.

Let us assume that we need 173,000 more women to fill the estimated shortfall in STEM. Is that a realistic aim? It would mean an increase of 26% more women in STEM. Even then, the percentage of women working in STEM would rise from 4.3% to only 5.4%, well below the 13.2% of men engaged in STEM. As a first step, can teachers inspire more girls into STEM?

Can teachers inspire more girls into STEM?

The following graphs show the numbers of boys and girls taking STEM A levels in England over the 10 years to 2022 (16):

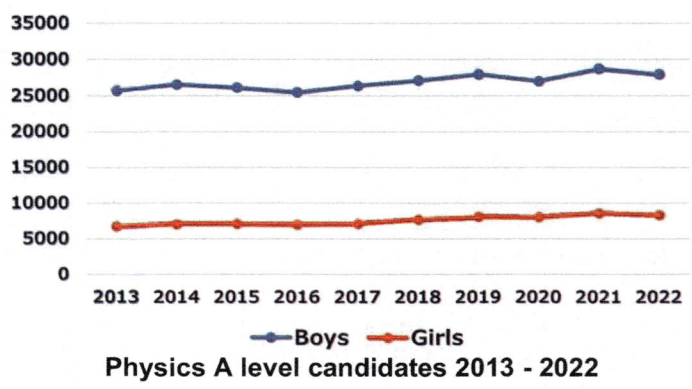

Physics A level candidates 2013 - 2022

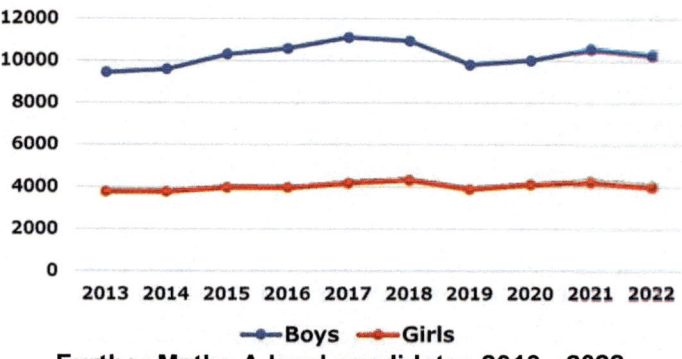

Further Maths A level candidates 2013 - 2022

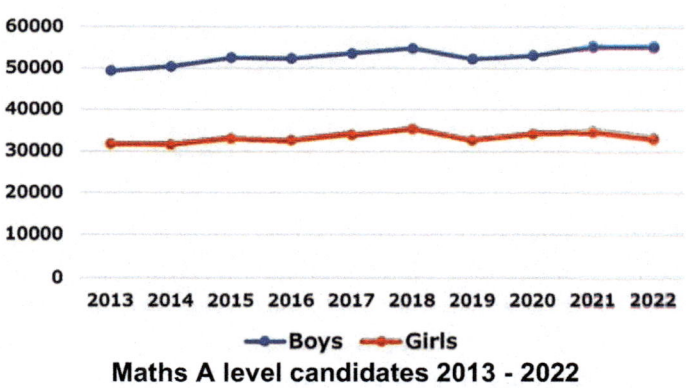

Maths A level candidates 2013 - 2022

Computing A level candidates 2013 - 2022

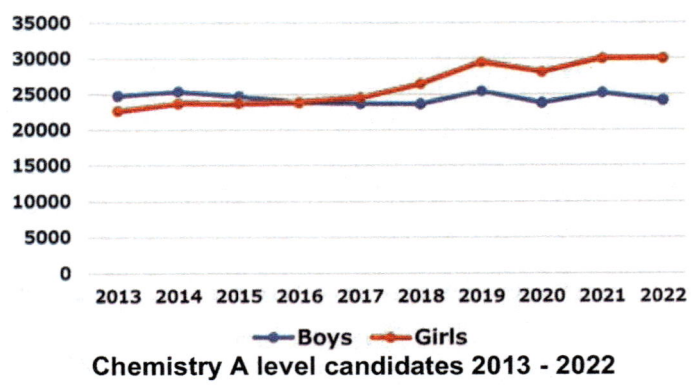

Chemistry A level candidates 2013 - 2022

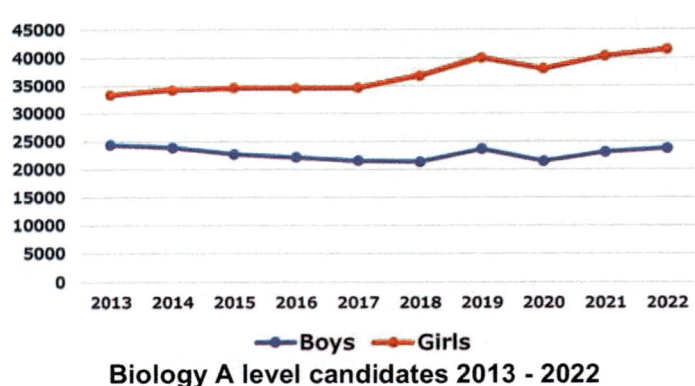

Biology A level candidates 2013 - 2022

When we sum all six STEM A levels, we still get a gap:

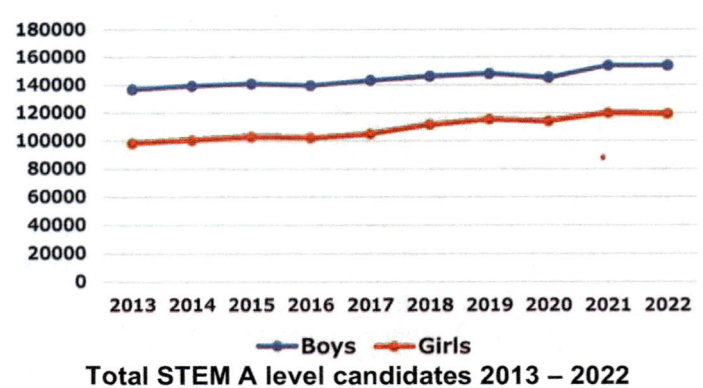

Total STEM A level candidates 2013 – 2022

The numbers of girls in England taking physics, further maths, and maths have remained flat over the years. The numbers of girls taking computing, chemistry, and biology have been gradually increasing for many years.

The Total STEM curve shows that more girls are taking STEM A levels, but the trend is so gradual that a shortfall of 173,000 women might not be filled until 2100. This is despite a concerted effort over the last decade or so to get girls into STEM. Inspiring more girls to take STEM A levels, whilst admirable, does not seem to be the answer to filling such a shortfall in the near future.

Purely on the basis of her physics class, Katharine Birbalsingh was accused of failing to inspire her girls to work in STEM. However, the graphs show that Birbalsingh's classes were in line with national trends. Her girls were in the minority in computing, further maths, and physics, but in in the majority in chemistry and biology. They bucked the national trend by being the majority in maths. Overall, Birbalsingh was not failing to inspire girls to take up STEM.

Following the backlash Birbalsingh hardened her stance. She tweeted: 'I am not going to force our girls to do A level physics if they don't want to do to it. It is OK if we don't have an exact gender balance in all subjects.' In that tweet, Birbalsingh went to the heart of the matter.

Birbalsingh's critics think in terms of identity diversity and gender balance. Birbalsingh thinks in terms of cognitive diversity and thinking preferences, irrespective of background and gender.

Birbalsingh knows that her girls are in the majority in maths, biology, and chemistry. If her girls are in the minority in physics and further maths, she accepts that as a fact of life and a natural outcome.

Can teachers inspire girls into STEM trades?

So far, we have covered STEM as being white-collar jobs at director, professional, and technician levels requiring degrees. However, some women work in blue-collar trades at the interface where intellectual STEM meets the real practical world: in what I will call STEM trades. These are hands-on occupations requiring technical vocational qualifications and skills training such as City & Guilds, NVQs, Apprenticeships and Accredited Certification Schemes, rather than degree level in-depth knowledge.

In the UK in 2022 skilled metal, electrical and electronic trades occupations comprised 6% of all men, and only 0.3% of all women (18). However, women in wartime quickly learned to perform these occupations.

One of my favourite paintings is *Ruby Loftus Screwing a Breech Ring* by Dame Laura Knight. 21-year-old Ruby became famous for very quickly mastering this tricky skill, 'usually practised by men with eight years' experience'. She is featured in a fascinating wartime newsreel on YouTube, viewing her portrait in the Royal Academy. The painting now hangs in the Imperial War Museum in Lambeth, and wonderfully evokes the atmosphere of a machine shop.

Here is an area that has very few women, but I am not aware of a clamour for teachers to inspire girls into STEM trades.

Can anyone else inspire girls into STEM?

Let's assume we are thinking of inspiring only the girls who take STEM A levels. We are not going to try to inspire the girls who do not take STEM A levels.

Let's assume we are thinking of inspiring girls in the school setting, away from their home life, where they may already be influenced to follow the family tradition, in medicine for example. Let's also assume that a role for teachers is to invite role models into the classroom to inspire pupils in person. Role models, who are working in STEM and living proof that perseverance pays off, who can galvanise girls into setting goals. For example, a two year goal to get excellent A Levels, a five year goal to get a good STEM degree, and possibly a longer term goal with a particular career in mind.

Since I have a strong interest in upward social mobility, I hope that female STEM role models who have overcome disadvantages will come forward. Some girls can believe themselves to be disadvantaged in one or more aspects of identity diversity, such as sex, ethnicity, disability, religion, poverty, or class. However, if they see women who have overcome such disadvantages, then they can be inspired to persevere and work hard for success. (All of this applies to boys, too).

But identity diversity is not the whole story. It is important for role models to speak publicly to reveal the quality of their minds. In science for example, who can fail to be inspired by women such as Dame Sarah Gilbert, Professor of Vaccinology at Oxford, and co-designer of the Oxford COVID-19 vaccine. Anyone who hears Professor Gilbert speak is bound to be inspired by her total professionalism.

Are women choosing to work outside STEM?

Katharine Birbalsingh's critics should beware what they wish for. The girls being inspired to take STEM A levels may not end up working in STEM. They may take up alternative careers instead. Could they account for the 173,000 workers estimated to be missing from STEM in 2021?

The next two tables compare career choices in the UK in 2022 for women with a strong preference for analytical thinking.

The first table shows women who chose to work in STEM (18):

	Occupations in STEM	Women in the occupation	% of all working women
Directors, Executives	Technology	29,800	0.2%
Professionals	Science	152,700	1.0%
	Technology	245,100	1.6%
	Engineering	65,100	0.4%
Technicians	Science	25,000	0.2%
	Technology	65,900	0.4%
	Engineering	77,300	0.5%
Totals		660,900	4.3%

Analytical women working in STEM in the UK in 2022

The second table shows women who chose to work outside STEM (18):

	Occupations outside STEM	Women in the occupation	% of all working women
Directors, Executives	Health, Finance	183,100	1.2%
Professionals	Health	364,300	2.3%
	Business	295,600	1.9%
	Finance	248,300	1.6%
	Legal	192,500	1.2%
Technicians	Health	100,000	0.6%
	Business	152,500	1.0%
	Finance	681,800	4.4%
Totals		2,218,100	14.2%

Analytical women working outside STEM in the UK in 2022

Hence, in 2022 there were more than three times as many such women working outside STEM (14.2%) than working in STEM (4.3%). Why is this? I think that there are two main reasons: the overall thinking preferences of women, and the social aspects.

Firstly, let us consider the overall thinking preferences of women. Cognitive Diversity At Work™ shows that there are twice as many women than men combining strong preferences for analytical and relational thinking:

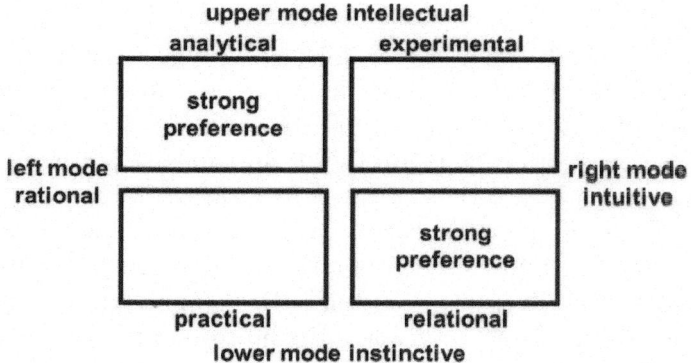

This profile is more attracted to health and service industries than STEM

Attributes of relational thinking include coaching, teaching, caring, nurturing, wellbeing, communication, and emotional empathy. Looked at from the *upper left* corner, women can be drawn to analytical careers that have a relational input. Hence, they can be drawn to careers in health, business, finance, and law rather than STEM.

Likewise, looked at from the *lower right* corner, women can be drawn to relational careers that have an analytical input. Hence, they can be drawn to careers in teaching physics and hard maths.

According to the *gov.uk* schoolteacher workforce statistics, some 75% of teachers are women, with more female than male teachers in every ethnic group. I surmise that MPs Moran and Monaghan have strong relational thinking preferences whereby they chose to teach physics rather than to work in STEM, and then moved into public service as politicians caring for their constituents.

Secondly, let us explore the possible social reasons why there are three times as many analytical women working outside STEM. Health, business, finance, and legal probably offer better pay, pensions, working conditions, prestige, social standing, and reputation than STEM.

They probably offer better job security because they are services which are in steady, constant, and lifelong demand by people. With only domestic competition, they practically guarantee a comfortable job for life and an excellent pension.

On a personal note, that was not my experience in aeronautical engineering, which is the most difficult of engineering degrees. Within the engineering sector, aeronautical engineering was at the bottom of the pay league.

I got an inkling of that during my first summer vacation at university, when I had to turn down an offer of work experience at British Aircraft Corporation Weybridge, because the wage would not even cover my accommodation expenses. Instead, I got double the money at the Sunblest bakery in Bradford, whilst living at home for free.

Yet, I persevered and, after my Short Service Commission in the RAF, absolutely loved working at Hawker Siddeley/British Aerospace Kingston on Harrier and Sea Harrier projects. However, with a large mortgage, sky high interest rates, and a young family to support, I simply could not make ends meet.

Therefore, I gave up a career that I loved to work in software systems, with an immediate 50% pay rise. I was able to pay off the credit cards, and we could afford to go on holiday for the first time in years!

Many STEM jobs can be subject to global market forces and job insecurity. This is typical of post-industrial societies such as the UK. For example, at least three of the world class STEM companies I have worked in – British Aerospace Kingston, Plessey Addlestone, and Thales Wells – are now housing estates.

Hence, Cognitive Diversity At Work™ explains why many women who have a strong preference for analytical thinking are choosing to work outside STEM in health, business, finance, and law rather than in STEM. They do so despite pressure in society to get more women into STEM, and I believe they do so for two reasons: the influence of their relational thinking, and the lifestyle rewards.

Chapter 17: The UK's Handling of COVID-19

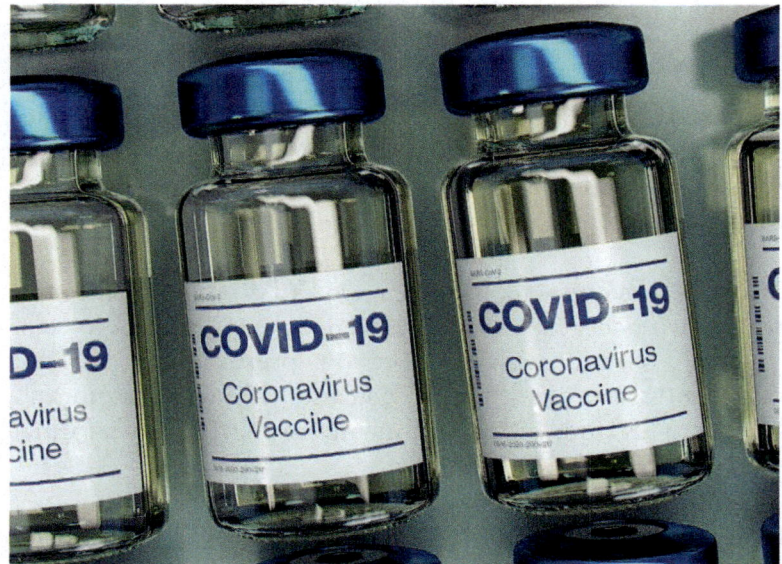

Finding insights

The aim of this chapter is to construct a cognitive diversity profile of the UK's handling of the COVID-19 pandemic. Using that profile, I will recommend which areas of thinking need to be changed to face a future pandemic. By 'UK' I mean the combination of SAGE, COBRA, and the Government Executive.

To collect the evidence for constructing a profile I quote independent experts who made insightful comments on the UK's handling of the crisis. I then look for examples of cognitive diversity in their insights. These are labelled in italics *upper left, lower left, lower right,* or *upper right.* From these examples I construct a pro-forma cognitive diversity profile of the UK's response to the pandemic.

Of course, readers may be aware of other evidence that they feel may paint a different picture. Readers are most welcome to send relevant evidence to md@cognitivediversity.co.uk.

By way of context, the death toll from COVID-19, compared with other causes of death, for all countries worldwide is shown on a live app (20). By 1 April 2024, the website showed for the UK 232,112 deaths from 24,910,387 cases. At times, COVID-19 has been the UK's biggest killer.

The UK government inquiry into COVID-19 is currently taking evidence. Its terms of reference are: 'The Inquiry will examine, consider and report on preparations and the response to the pandemic in England, Wales, Scotland and Northern Ireland, up to and including the Inquiry's formal setting-up date, 28 June 2022'.

No UK strategic plan for a coronavirus pandemic

Samuel Lovett reported in *The Independent* that the UK had no strategic plan *(avoiding upper right)* for dealing with a coronavirus pandemic.

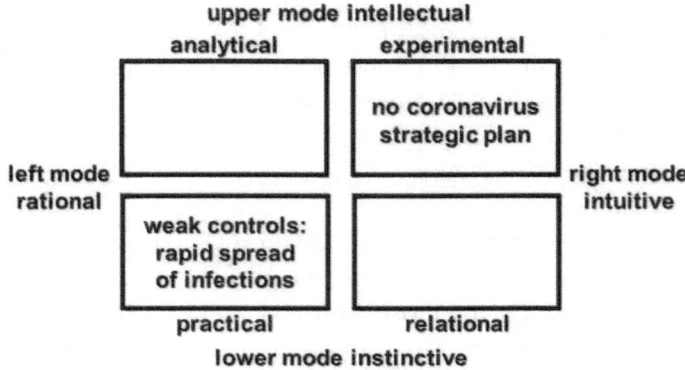

No UK strategic plan for a coronavirus pandemic

From February 2020 the UK loosely followed a strategy devised for tackling an influenza pandemic. Since influenza is far less dangerous than a coronavirus, mass gatherings were allowed, international arrivals from affected countries were not quarantined, and the virus was permitted to transmit through the population *(all weak lower left)*.

However, Lovett revealed that the UK did have a draft strategic plan for a coronavirus. It was written in 2005 and was filed away and forgotten *(avoiding upper right strategic thinking)*. It only came to light following a Freedom of Information request in 2021.

The 48-page document was based on the UK response to the 2003 SARS coronavirus pandemic. It included measures that were eventually adopted against COVID-19, but only after great loss of life, and with serious damage to social, health, educational, and economic wellbeing *(avoiding lower right relational thinking)*.

Sir David King, chief scientific adviser from 2000 to 2007, who was involved in developing the 2005 draft, said: "The SARS contingency plan should have been used instead of the 'flu textbook at the beginning of the COVID-19 pandemic. It was overlooked. I believe tens of thousands of lives would have been saved. I think the economy would have been in a much better place too."

By contrast, Sweden did have a strategic plan off-the-shelf and used it from day one.

One wonders if the authors of the 2005 plan tried telling SAGE, COBRA, and the Executive in early 2020 of its existence. If they did try, did groupthink prevent them from being listened to?

The UK's border controls

The research team of global health governance at Canada's Simon Fraser University in Burnaby found that, for cross-border measures to work against a pandemic, they need to be applied early on. The islands of Taiwan and Hong Kong did

apply them early by imposing the first border controls on 31 December 2019.
Prof Devi Sridhar, chair of global public health at the University of Edinburgh, said that when dealing with a pandemic: "To be an island in 2020 or 2021 is probably the greatest geographical gift you could have." Did the UK make the best use of its natural gift as an island?

Two alternative approaches for the UK were possible. Either very strong external border controls limited to essential traffic (combined with normal internal public health measures) resulting in more or less normal life; or weak border controls allowing non-essential traffic such as international holidays (combined with very strong public health measures) resulting in very restricted life.

The UK confirmed its first case of COVID-19 on 31 January 2020. Some travel measures were introduced but then withdrawn on 13 March 2020, with no further border measures *(weak lower left)* in place until 8 June 2020. Genetic analysis revealed that COVID-19 was individually introduced into the UK well over a thousand times during early 2020 – mostly from Spain, France, and Italy, which are popular with UK holiday makers.

Multiple chains of transmission were initiated in parallel from multiple points of entry to all four corners of the UK. This rapidly overwhelmed the UK's existing capacity for individual-level contact tracing. The virus was not cordoned off at points of entry. The UK did not introduce strong border quarantine controls *(strong lower left)* until as late as February 2021.

Hence, the UK's initial response was weak external border controls *(weak lower left)* but without very strong internal public health measures *(weak lower left)*. It seems that the UK did not make best use of its natural gift of being an island.

SAGE advice to the UK Government

The Scientific Advisory Group for Emergencies (SAGE) comprises some 86 eminent scientists. SAGE was responsible for ensuring that timely and coordinated scientific advice *(strong upper left)* was given to the UK Government decision makers, when required. Decision makers met in the Cabinet Office Briefing Room A (COBR A) and the meetings were known as COBRA.

Throughout the pandemic, SAGE was chaired by the Government Chief Scientific Adviser Sir Patrick Vallance and co-chaired by the Chief Medical Officer Professor Chris Whitty. Sir Patrick Vallance represented SAGE at the COBRA meetings.

When the Prime Minister briefed on COVID-19, he was usually flanked by Messrs. Vallance and Whitty. This visually reinforced the widely held belief that Government policy on COVID-19 was 'following the science' and driven by SAGE's strongly analytical *(strong upper left)* thinking. This begs the question as to how much weight the Government attached to the economic *(lower left)*, social, health, and educational *(lower right)*, and strategic *(upper right)* factors.

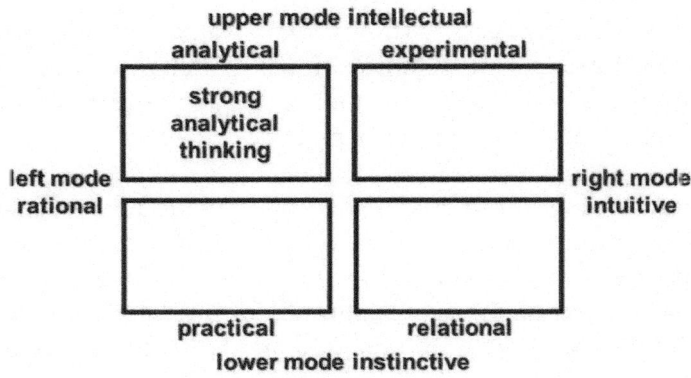

UK Government 'following the science'

Dame Helena Morrissey, financier and campaigner wrote: 'However admirable their work, SAGE are hired to advise rather than dictate. Their word is not gospel. Their individual opinions are often fiercely contested by colleagues and many of their analyses have turned out to be flawed.'

She continued: 'More importantly, they have a vested interest in playing up the worst-case scenarios, as they don't want to be accused of complacency. So, SAGE should include other experts to challenge and provide different perspectives, such as mental health practitioners *(lower right)*, cancer specialists *(upper left)* and, dare I say it, economists *(lower left)*, too.'

In August 2022, in an interview with The Spectator magazine, Rishi Sunak MP said it was wrong to "empower scientists" to such a degree during the pandemic. He said he believed that one of the major mistakes of the pandemic was to allow SAGE to have so much sway over policy.

The role of 'nudging' in stoking fears

In addition to SAGE, the Cabinet, and COBRA there was the influential BIT (Behavioural Insights Team). BIT has been accused of 'nudging' public opinion and behaviour so that the public was more compliant. A group of 40 psychologists have written to Parliament's Public Administration and Constitutional Affairs Committee, warning that BIT was unaccountable *(avoiding lower left)* and unethical *(avoiding lower right)*.

The psychologists opposed the use of dramatic adverts, which included slogans such as: 'If you go out you can spread it, people will die' *(avoiding lower right)*. They condemned the use of 'images of the acutely unwell in intensive care units' *(avoiding lower right)* on billboard and television adverts.

The signatories said it was "…highly questionable whether a civilised society should knowingly increase the emotional discomfort *(avoiding lower right)* of its citizens as a means of gaining their compliance". The letter drew attention to a government memo from March 2020, which suggested that '...the perceived level of personal threat needs to be increased among those who are complacent' and called for more frightening messaging *(avoiding lower right)*.

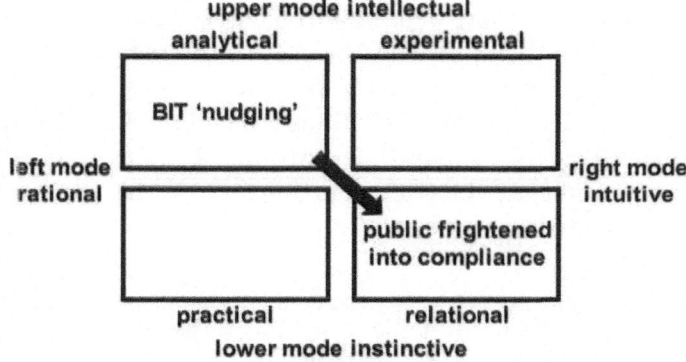

**The BIT was accused of 'nudging'
the public into compliance**

Lord Sumption, a former British supreme court justice, wrote: 'The worst aspect has been the misuse (by SAGE) of statistical modelling to project extravagant figures for future deaths...the use of statements such as these is not designed to inform, but to scare Ministers into taking abrasive measures and to scare *(avoiding lower right)* the public into supporting them.'

'Everyone is at risk'

At a briefing in March 2020, cabinet minister Michael Gove warned that the virus did not discriminate by announcing: "Everyone is at risk." Prof Mark Woolhouse, professor of infectious disease epidemiology at the Usher Institute at the University of Edinburgh, a mathematical modeller, and a member of the UK Scientific Pandemic Influenza Group on Modelling (Spi-M), wrote that '...nothing could be further from the truth' (21).

He explained: "I am afraid Gove's statement was simply not true. In fact, this is a very discriminatory virus. Some people are much more at risk from it than others. People over 75 are an astonishing 10,000 times more at risk than those who are under 15."

At this juncture it may be useful to have some understanding of the word 'risk'. The concept of risk is largely misunderstood in society. However, project management has a very clear understanding of risk management. A project risk is measured by the dimensionless product P times I, where P is the probability of the risk occurring and I is the impact if it does occur. Society tends to think of a risk only in terms of its impact.

For example, town councillors in Cornwall banned daffodils from a local recreation ground – for fear that children could make themselves ill by eating them. The town councillors considered only the impact. They did not consider that the chances of children snacking on daffodils is practically zero: Google shows no evidence of children anywhere in the world eating daffodils. Council bureaucrats clearly think differently.

As a project manager and project risk manager from industry I taught both specialisms at Portsmouth University to business executives. Projects use the Probability Impact Diagram (PID) to decide where to allocate scarce resources in mitigation. Risk mitigation reduces the probability that a certain risk will occur and if it does occur it tries to reduce the impacts due to it.

The Probability Impact Diagram at the start of the pandemic, before any mitigation, shows that everyone – children, workers, the elderly, frail and infirm – were at High probability of catching COVID-19. We now know that the impact of catching COVID-19 ranged from Low for children to High for the elderly, frail, and infirm.

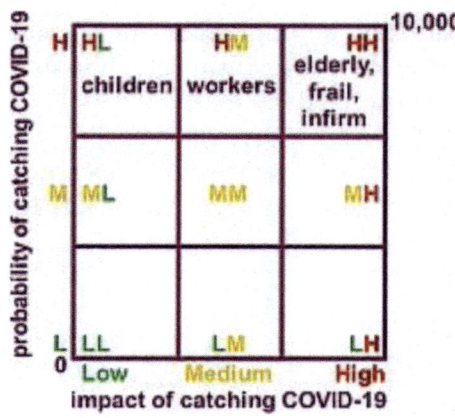

Probability Impact Diagram at the start of COVID-19

In the absence of vaccines, mitigation would be limited to reducing the probability of catching the virus. For the elderly, frail, and infirm public health interventions can reduce the probability of catching the virus from High to Low or near zero. Whilst the impact of catching the virus could still be serious or fatal, the overall risk would be reduced from High–High to Low–High:

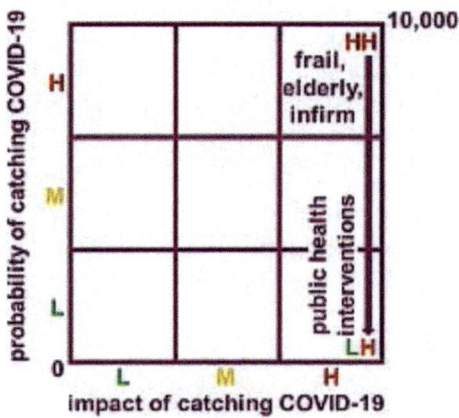

**Public health interventions reduce
the chances of catching COVID-19**

Vaccination can reduce the risk from High–High to High–Low; although the probability of catching the virus could be

High, its impact may be unpleasant but not fatal. I had fully vaxxed frail, elderly, or infirm neighbours who caught COVID-19 and survived.

The PID below shows how vaccinations reduce the impact and thereby the overall risk of catching COVID-19.

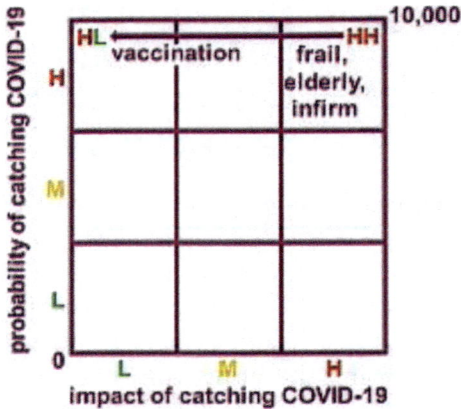

Vaccinations reduce the impact of COVID-19

Everyone was not at the same level of risk

Research shows that COVID-19 differentiates between the old and young. Data (22) shows that, of the 50,335 deaths involving COVID-19 occurring between March and June 2020 in England and Wales, 45,859 (91.1%) of the victims had pre-existing medical conditions such as dementia and Alzheimer's disease, ischaemic heart diseases, influenza, and pneumonia. 47,036 of the 50,335 (93.4%) were of retirement age.

Overall, the victims were overwhelmingly the elderly and those with pre-existing conditions which suggests that people of working age, without underlying pre-existing medical conditions, are relatively safe, and the younger you are, the safer you are. The risk of infection of course exists in multi-generational households.

Analysis in 2022 (22) by the ONS showed that mortality was higher for people aged 30 to 64 who were obese, than those who were not. The rate of death involving COVID-19 was over two times greater for obese men and women compared with those of a healthy weight. The higher rates were consistent even when adjusted for age, ethnic group, smoking status, and vaccination status. Analysis of the graphs of UK cases and deaths leads me to the following conclusions.

In the spring 2020 surge there was little or no testing available and the number of cases exceeding the number of deaths were simply those who clearly had COVID-19 but survived. The correlation between spring 2020 deaths and numbers of cases was strong: one death per six infected (17%).

In the autumn/winter 2020 surge, when testing was widely available, the cases were anyone who tested positive. However, I have seen no differentiation between positive cases such as: those with no symptoms, those with mild symptoms, those with real symptoms who recovered at home, those severe cases who were admitted to hospital and recovered, and those admitted to intensive care and recovered.

The correlation between autumn/winter 2020 deaths and numbers of cases was not strong (typically, one death per 50 infected). Nevertheless, the Government ordered the indiscriminate, nationwide autumn/winter 2020 lockdowns 2 and 3 *(very strong lower left control)*.

In mid-June 2021, NHS England did start to discriminate by instructing hospitals to change the daily flow of data. The change differentiated between those in hospital for COVID-19 and those who simply tested positive while seeking treatment for something else. NHS England told *The Independent* that the move was being done to help analyse the effect of the vaccine programme and whether it was successfully reducing COVID-19 sickness.

The first wave and lockdown 1

In March 2020 SAGE advised a scenario in which there would be 510,000 deaths from the virus if the Government took no action. That is a figure higher than all British deaths, service and civilian, in the six years of the Second World War.

The Government took this advice as justification for the first lockdown. As the Prime Minister said, the UK Government "…is following the science" *(strong upper left)*. Lockdown reduces the probability of catching the virus from high to low, as in the PID diagram.

On 23rd March 2020, the Prime Minister announced lockdown 1 in his televised address: "From this evening I must give the British people a very simple instruction - you must stay at home."

Places of work, education and leisure - including restaurants, bars, pubs, cinemas, nightclubs, theatres, gyms, leisure centres, libraries, playgrounds, outdoor gyms, and places of worship - were forced to close.

Meeting friends or family members who did not live with you was prohibited *(strong lower left and avoiding lower right)*. 'Hands, face, space' - hand washing, wearing masks, and social distancing - became the norm *(strong lower left)*.

The PM also said, "To put it simply, if too many people become seriously unwell at one time, the NHS will be unable to handle it - meaning more people are likely to die, not just from Coronavirus but from other illnesses as well."

It was most unfortunate, but I sensed that the PM's statement caused fear and alarm in equal measure *(avoiding lower right)*. I could recall no other Prime Minister at a time of national emergency ever saying that people were going to die.

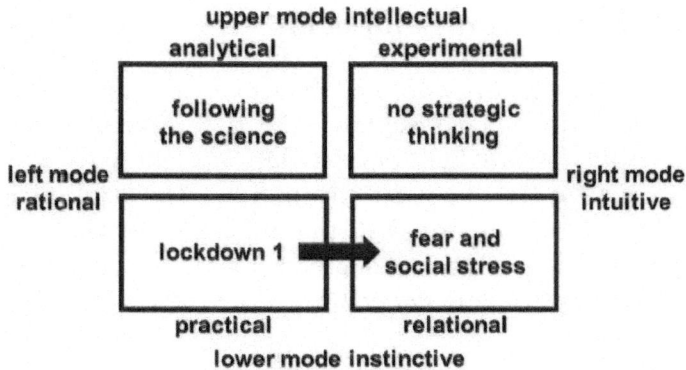

**Surging infection rates led to
lockdown 1 from 23 March 2020**

Even Winston Churchill in June 1940, after the fall of France when the UK faced the possibility of invasion by Nazi Germany, never said anything like: "To put it simply, if we stand up to Hitler, more people are likely to die, not just soldiers but civilians as well."

What Churchill did talk about instead was a future time *(upper right)* when "...the life of the world may move forward into broad, sunlit uplands." That was an overarching goal *(upper right),* beyond the current problems, that inspired, motivated, gave hope, - and stopped people being afraid.

People like Joan Seaman, a London civilian in 1940, who said: "I remember being very frightened indeed when France collapsed because I thought it was going to be us next. Really frightened. Until I heard the speech *(lower right communication)* that Churchill made on the radio about fighting on the beaches. I suddenly wasn't frightened any more. It was quite amazing. When people have decried Churchill, I've always said he stopped me being afraid!" (23).

Without doubt, there is much evidence to show that Winston Churchill practised cognitive diversity, long before it was given the name.

Hospitals close to breaking point

In her book *Breathtaking,* hospital palliative care doctor Dr Rachel Clarke described hospitals close to breaking point (24). She wrote much of her book off-duty at night when she 'couldn't sleep for fear, fury, and frustration'. She attributed her fury and frustration largely to the 'inadequacies and lies of politicians', the delays in decisions, and the 'number theatre' of statistics *(strong upper left).*

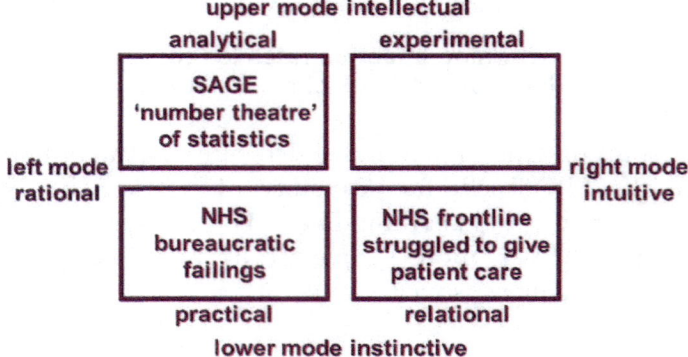

upper mode intellectual

analytical	experimental
SAGE 'number theatre' of statistics	
NHS bureaucratic failings	**NHS frontline** struggled to give patient care

left mode rational   **right mode intuitive**

practical   **relational**

lower mode instinctive

The first wave contrasted SAGE thinking and NHS bureaucracy with frontline care

In his book *Intensive Care,* General Practitioner Dr Gavin Francis wrote of the GP surgeries struggling with a surge in patient mental-health crises (25).

Their books starkly contrasted the SAGE-led thinking *(upper left)* of the Government and the NHS management bureaucracy *(lower left),* with the caring thinking *(lower right)* of the NHS frontline clinical workers.

Whilst noting the failings of the NHS bureaucracy, Doctors Clarke and Francis praised those on the frontline of healthcare who struggled against the odds to give every patient attention and kindness *(strong lower right).* They argued that strong relationships – trust, warmth, and kindness *(strong lower right)* – are not pleasant extras but are absolutely essential to healthcare.

Both authors reminded the policymakers and politicians that the quest for efficiency, improved productivity, and an audit culture *(lower left management)* in the NHS has too often destroyed relationships *(avoiding lower right)*. Do the NHS management metrics quantify care, kindness, and compassion?

I am reminded of when my mother was admitted to hospital with terminal cancer. A senior nurse came over and whispered an apology over a lack of care and compassion, saying, "I'm sorry, it's just about money and budgets now," and that was in 1997, more than a quarter of a century ago.

The second wave and lockdowns 2 and 3

It was reported that SAGE graphs, which predicted 50,000 cases a day by mid-October 2020 and 4,000 deaths a day by late November 2020, were used by Downing Street in a hastily organised press conference to justify England's lockdown 2 starting 5 November 2020. Within hours, the UK Statistics Authority condemned the figure of 4,000.

Eminent Cambridge statistician Professor Sir David Spiegelhalter was quoted as saying that Number 10 cherry-picked worst-case scenarios and 'spurious' COVID-19 data *(upper left)* to justify England's lockdown 2 *(strong lower left)* and may have intended to frighten the public *(avoiding lower right)*.

In giving evidence to the House of Commons Public Administration and Constitutional Affairs Committee, Sir David said that ministers had "...broken pretty much every code of conduct by choosing only to show worst-case scenarios, which were often based on out-of-date data."

He continued: "I don't want to ascribe motivation to anyone of course. But if someone was really trying to manipulate *(lower left)* the audience and frighten them *(avoiding lower right)* and persuade them that what was being done was correct, rather than genuinely inform them, then this is the kind of thing they might do."

Even Conservative MPs compared the doomsday data, used to justify lockdown 2, to the controversial Labour government dossier that sent the UK to war in Iraq in 2003. That dossier claimed that Iraq could deploy weapons of mass destruction within 45 minutes. No such weapons of mass destruction were ever found in Iraq.

In an interview with Lisa O'Kelly of *The Observer*, Dr Rachel Clarke said. "In the first wave, the NHS threw all it had at trying to manage COVID-19, so everything else shut down. This time, the NHS has been desperately trying to catch up on all the other non-COVID-19 activity that was suspended, so staff have gone into the second wave already exhausted.

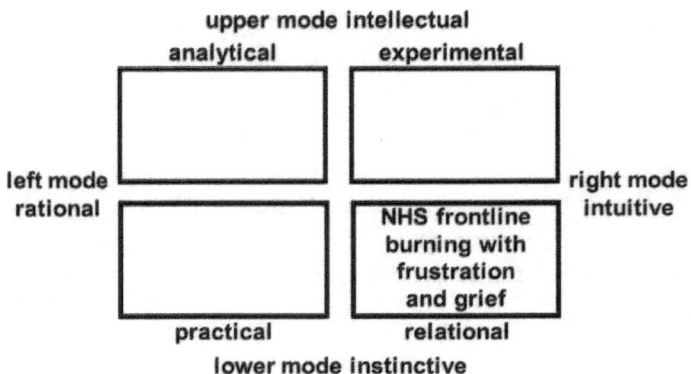

**NHS frontline staff went into
the second wave already exhausted**

"Many staff are suffering from clinical depression, anxiety, post-traumatic stress disorder. I've seen colleagues break down in tears in the hospital. We are also seeing younger patients, which is shocking. The most soul-destroying aspect of this second wave is to a very large extent this could have been prevented. Staff are just burning with frustration and grief *(avoiding lower right).*"

Lockdown 2 ended on 2 December 2020 and was followed by multi-tier restrictions resulting in lockdown 3 starting on 6 January 2021. The success of the subsequent vaccination rollout led to a gradual lifting of restrictions by late July 2021.

The social damage of lockdowns

By 31st March 2020, a significant rise in anxiety and depression among the UK population was reported. The study, by researchers from the University of Sheffield and Ulster University, found that people reporting anxiety increased from 17% to 36%, while those people reporting depression increased from 16% to 38%.

Dame Helena Morrissey wrote at the time that '...the continuing disproportionate focus on coronavirus created a persistent atmosphere of exaggerated fear; the pursuit of safety *(strong lower left)* became its own menace; on top of the economic damage, lockdowns brought a host of social problems, from fractured relationships *(avoiding lower right)* to an increase in excessive drinking.'

Dame Helena also described the profound feelings of alienation and oppression *(avoiding lower right)*, so different from the freedoms people took for granted until COVID-19. How the institutional obsession *(strong lower left)* with COVID-19 became all-consuming. How its authoritarianism *(strong lower left)* extended into every aspect of life. How lives were governed by an endless barrage of complex, sometimes contradictory edicts *(strong lower left)*.

There was mass rebellion against lockdown 1 as soon as it was eased from 1 June through to August 2020. Restrictions were then progressively re-applied through September and

October. On 14th September 2020 'The Rule of Six' was introduced to ban *(strong lower left)* social gatherings *(avoiding lower right)* of more than six people indoors or outdoors.

The rule was to be enforced *(strong lower left)* by roaming 'COVID-19 Marshals', with fines of up to £6,400, and the threat of a criminal record *(strong upper left)*. Neighbour was encouraged to inform on neighbour in the manner of a totalitarian state *(strong lower left control)*.

All the above, and much more, reflect *strong to very strong preferences in lower left thinking*, whilst avoiding *lower right relational thinking*.

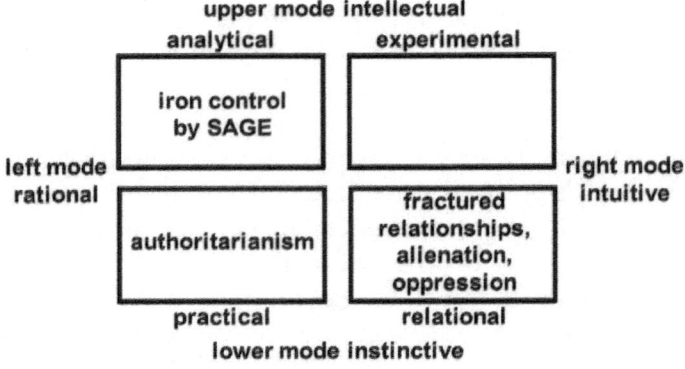

Social damage of lockdowns

Dame Helena warned that the UK needed to learn to live with the risks through a more balanced *(all four ways of thinking)* pragmatic policy that took account of the wider social and economic needs, and that ministers should break free from the iron control *(strong lower left)* exerted for too long by the scientists.

This is important, because a major study by the Institute for Fiscal Studies (IFS) and the UCL Institute of Education showed that lockdowns 'harmed the emotional development of almost half of children'. Parents said their children appeared more worried, had lost confidence more easily, and were more prone to tantrums and low moods after the UK's COVID-19 lockdowns. Interestingly, the study found no evidence that poorer children suffered any worse impact on their social and emotional skills than their wealthier peers.

It's also interesting to contrast the outcomes of children watching TV during peacetime lockdown, and children growing up during the Second World War. I recall speaking with work colleagues who were children during the war, and their experience is well illustrated in the 1987 film *Hope and Glory*. They coped and had the time of their lives. The difference that makes the difference is that they went to school, played with their chums outside school, had fun and carried on.

In December 2023 the COVID Inquiry was threatened with legal action over fears it was biased in favour of lockdowns. The children's rights campaign group UsForThem wrote to the Inquiry to demand it alters its scope to ensure harms caused by lockdown are properly examined.

The health damage of lockdowns

The Telegraph compiled a summary from sources including Cancer Research UK, NHS England, Royal College of Psychiatrists, British Heart Foundation, Office of National Statistics, and Carers UK. The summary showed how COVID-19 impacted NHS treatment in 2020:

- three million people in the UK missed cancer screenings as a result of coronavirus

- two million patients waited more than 18 weeks for routine hospital treatment

- one in ten mental health patients waited six months for help

- 50% drop in heart attack A&E attendances

- 38% drop in emergency heart surgery in London in the second half of March 2020, due to worried patients

- 50% of Britons reported high levels of anxiety

- 35% of carers provided more care as a result of local services reducing or closing.

In April 2022, *The Telegraph* reported that: 'Cancer patients paying for their chemotherapy privately would otherwise be dead; some 6.2 million people are on waiting lists for hospital treatment, which could top 11 million as more people who stayed at home during the pandemic come forward for care; GP appointments are rarer than hens' teeth; mental health support for young people is teetering on the brink of collapse; and the state of maternity services is iniquitous, terrifying, shameful.'

Dr Ellie Cannon, a General Practitioner, wrote that all doctors make a promise to protect *(strong lower right)* their patients from harm. She had become deeply concerned that, as a GP, she risked breaking that pledge. By not speaking out she felt that she risked being complicit in the Government's policies which, she claimed, were harming the country on two fronts.

Firstly, with the lion's share of NHS resources taken up by COVID-19, so many other areas of healthcare had fallen by the wayside *(avoiding lower right)*.

Secondly, her patients were anxious and depressed due to job loss, bereavement, and fear. They were scared of leaving the house by daily death bulletins, doom-laden predictions, and horrific Government adverts – echoes of stoking fears by 'nudging'.

She described the harm caused by lockdowns: suicides, the ultimate consequence of untreated mental health problems exacerbated by unemployment, money worries and the isolation and misery of lockdown measures; rising rates of child abuse injuries; and the declining physical health of the elderly. She summarised by claiming that the true health crisis facing the UK was the fault of the Government itself.

'Don't think for a minute I'd advocate letting the virus rip,' she continued. 'But there has to be a middle way – one in which we aren't trading one health threat for many others.' Could the Great Barrington Declaration 'Focused Protection' have been Dr Cannon's 'middle way'? Sub chapter 'Focused protection not lockdown' in this book covers the Great Barrington Declaration.

I conclude that, in following SAGE, the UK government was locked in *upper left* groupthink. Dr Cannon drew attention to the Government's lack of empathy, poor communications, and lack of protection from collateral harm in other areas of healthcare *(all avoiding lower right)*.

Karol Sikora, cancer specialist, professor of medicine at University of Buckingham Medical School and Chief Medical Officer at Rutherford Health, despaired at he called the collateral damage of Government policy: 'Thousands more people will die in the coming months and years because of undiagnosed cancers, cardiac disorders and other treatable conditions than will succumb directly to COVID-19.

'This Government has been very successful in the business of spreading fear about COVID-19, but in not much else. What people desperately need now is belief that things can, and will, get back to a state of being that they recognise. Above all, they crave that most human of emotion – a sense of hope *(upper right)*.'

Professor Sikora also cautioned against the adoption of 'telemedicine' – the idea that far more GP consultations should be done via video or phone. He wrote: 'Being in the room with the patient allows the doctor to get a far better understanding *(strong lower right)* and feel of what's going on. Nothing can replace an in-person appointment, and it's not a risk we should take.'

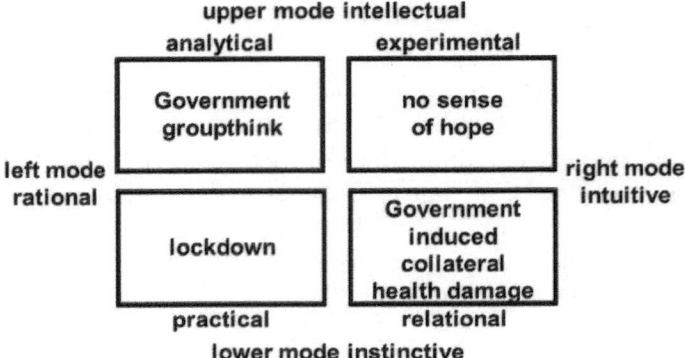

**Collateral health damage of lockdowns
induced by Government groupthink**

Sikora wrote that the COVID Inquiry '...ignored the one number that would blow lockdown out of the water. The Prime Minister Rishi Sunak highlighted a study of the first lockdown that suggested more quality adjusted life years (QALYs) would be taken by lockdown than the virus itself. Lead counsel to the inquiry Hugo Keith KC shut the Prime Minister down with unerring speed, stating that he was not interested in this approach'.

QALYs estimate how many years a certain intervention will save or take, including a calculation of the quality of that time. Sikora wrote that QALYs is the best metric we have for measuring the success or failure of various medical interventions in any resource-limited health system.

He observed that the bottom line in the cost-benefit analysis of the first lockdown in the UK, published in 2020, was negative in every scenario. In other words, the cure was worse than the disease - yet still more lockdowns were ordered.

In Sikora's opinion, the lives and wellbeing of the young were sacrificed to protect the elderly. He estimates that '...more life-years will be lost from delays in cancer diagnosis and treatment alone than were taken by the virus, and this is just one tiny fraction of lockdown's collateral damage'. Professor Sikora recommended that Mr Sunak's intervention should be the basis for an entirely new inquiry exploring a proper cost-benefit analysis of 2020-2021.

The education damage of lockdowns

In a written witness statement to the COVID Inquiry, Prime Minister Rishi Sunak stated that following the science during COVID had the 'unfortunate consequence' of lockdowns damaging both the economy and children's education. Yet I clearly recall that the mantra at the time was 'follow the science'.

The Prime Minister continued: 'Scientists are not perfect or incapable of error, and even as late as October 2020 there was a lack of evidence for what measures did and did not work. As a result, less consideration was given to the serious impacts of lockdowns on society'.

For children, there were direct and indirect impacts. In addition to the lost academic progress directly due from being absent from the classroom, there was also an indirect impact. Josh Hillman, the director of education at the Nuffield Foundation, has said: "Children's social and emotional development is important, not only in its own right but also in supporting their capacity to learn and achieve in school, which in turn can bolster their longer-term outcomes."

One can imagine the following scenario: lockdown results in a drop in social and emotional development, which results in a drop in capacity to learn and achieve. After lockdown, time is required to rebuild social and emotional development, and the related capacity to learn and achieve.

Hence, the impact of lockdown continues to be felt after lockdown. Maybe this can be read across to adults at work; maybe working from home reduces productivity.

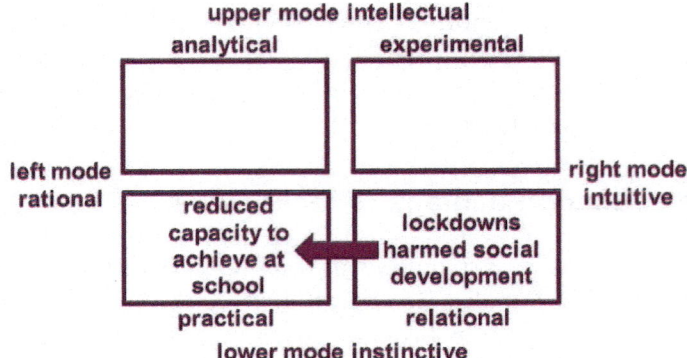

Indirect educational damage to children of lockdowns

The economic damage of lockdowns

The UK Government forecast the following:

- National Debt to exceed a record £2,000bn; unemployment to peak at 7.75% in the second quarter of 2021, equal to 2.65 million people out of work; business investment to drop some 19%; the economy to shrink 11% – the worst performance in living memory, including the Second World War. By comparison, at the worst of the 2008 financial crisis, the economy shrank by 'only' 5%

- total 'Quantitative Easing' to total some £895bn. QE is the Bank of England creating digital money to buy things like government debt in the form of bonds with the aim of boosting spending and investment in the economy. Reports stated that a side effect would see savers punished for their prudence by seeing their nest eggs diluted

- revenues from corporation tax, income tax, National Insurance, fuel duties and VAT to plunge whilst Government spending to soar by some 30% as costs of dealing with COVID-19 mounted.

In September 2021 the National Audit Office (NAO) estimated the total cost of Government COVID-19 support measures as £370bn comprising: £154bn for businesses; £84bn for health and social care; £67bn for other public services and emergency responses; £60bn for individuals; and £5bn for other support and operational expenditure. That compared with total government spending of £853bn in pre-COVID 2018-19. All of this has to be paid for.

In the Spring Statement of 2022, the Chancellor of the Exchequer introduced the biggest tax hike since the 1940s, perpetuating the worst squeeze on living standards since the 1950s. Inflation for March 2022 at 7% - excluding higher energy costs from 1 April - was the highest figure recorded since 1992.

The NAO warned of leakage of some £30bn out of the support measures comprising: £26bn from business support through fraud, organised crime, and borrowers going bust; £4bn from employee furlough support though criminals and dodgy employers; and hundreds of millions of pounds from the £10.8bn spent on PPE contracts awarded without competitive tender. £8.7bn was wasted on below standard personal protective equipment (PPE).

Some 20,000 shops closed down, with 235,000 High Street retail employees thrown out of work. Many came from high-profile redundancy rounds at the likes of Boots (4,000), John Lewis (2,400), Debenhams (6,500), and Arcadia (13,000).

Economic damage has knock-on effects. Commentators report the social and health fallouts from economic damage include fear, worry, anxiety, stress, depression, self-harm, domestic violence, crime, distress, misery, loss of hope, hopelessness, lack of self-worth *(all counter to lower right relational thinking)*. They in turn will impede economic recovery.

It is a vicious circle. I can personally vouch for the total misery of redundancy and unemployment and understand why some people can retreat into a very, very dark place. President Roosevelt broke the vicious circle of fear in America at the height of the Great Depression in 1933 by saying: "...the only thing we have to fear is...fear itself."

Dr David Nabarro, the World Health Organisation's Special Envoy on COVID-19, said in November 2020: "We really do appeal to all world leaders: stop using lockdown as your primary control method. Lockdowns have one consequence that you can never belittle, and that is making poor people an awful lot poorer."

Lord Sumption, a former British supreme court justice, wrote that SAGE was '...transfixed by containing transmission of the virus, even though this is only part of the issue. The truth is that there is always a trade-off to be made between the damage done by COVID-19 and the damage from countermeasures.

'A lack of balance *(a lack of strong thinking in all four quadrants)* and proportion have been an abiding feature of Government policy from the outset. In April 2020, Ministers formulated five tests which would guide policy, none of which took account of the social, economic, or psychological costs *(counter to lower right)*.

'In his press conference on May 10, 2020, the Prime Minister proudly declared that the Government would "...not be driven by economic necessity" – as if the population's livelihoods were of no importance.'

Lord Sumption continued: 'As a parliamentary committee reported in July 2020, there has never been a proper impact assessment or cost-benefit analysis to assess the wider effects on our society'.

Professor Chris Whitty, the Chief Medical Officer, told a Commons committee that the measures taken to suppress the virus '...are economically and socially destructive' *(counter to lower right)*, but it was not his job to think about that.' In saying that, Professor Whitty demonstrated that he was avoiding *lower right* thinking.

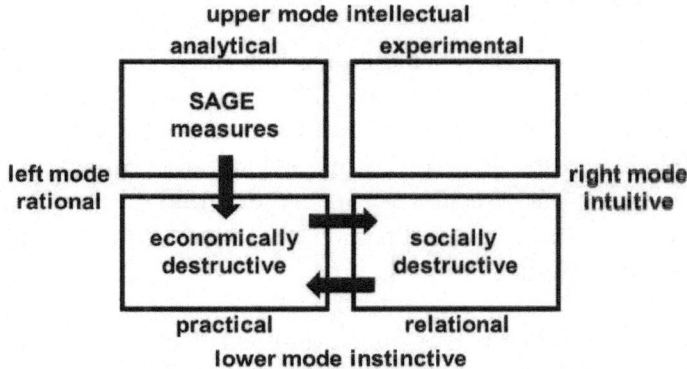

Chief Medical Officer:
'SAGE measures are economically and socially destructive'

In May 2022, Juliet Samuel commented in *The Telegraph* that, far from being harmless and manageable, the vast expansion in state spending and monetary policy trialled by COVID policies had profoundly damaging effects on the cost of living, the security of public finances, the resilience, and working culture of the UK.

The OECD reported in February 2024 that the impact of lockdown on children risked damaging productivity for decades. 'Lockdowns threaten to wipe £700bn off the global economy and stunt growth for decades because of the lasting impact of school closures on young people. A marked deterioration in basic reading and writing skills among 15-year-olds since 2018 would damage the earnings potential of a generation of school leavers for most of their working lives.'

Jeremy Warner, one of the UK's foremost financial, economic and business journalists, writing in *The Telegraph* summed up as follows: 'Both in terms of its impact on economic output and its fiscal costs, the pandemic and the response to it appear to have inflicted more damage on the UK than almost any other advanced economy. This for no obvious advantage in terms of public health outcomes'.

'Focused Protection not lockdown'

In 2020, there was growing concern at the devastating effects of lockdowns. On 4 October 2020, the Great Barrington Declaration (26) was authored and signed by Dr. Martin Kulldorff, professor of medicine at Harvard University, Dr. Sunetra Gupta, professor in epidemiology at Oxford University, and Dr. Jay Bhattacharya, a professor at Stanford University Medical School.

By August 2024 it had attracted 940,332 signatures across the world of 876,459 concerned citizens, 16,135 medical & public health scientists, and 47,738 medical practitioners. I signed as a concerned citizen.

The Declaration stated: 'Current lockdown policies are producing devastating effects on short and long-term public health. The results (to name a few) include lower childhood vaccination rates, worsening cardiovascular disease outcomes, fewer cancer screenings and deteriorating mental health – leading to greater excess mortality in years to come, with the working class and younger members of society carrying the heaviest burden.

'Keeping students out of school is a grave injustice. Keeping these measures in place until a vaccine is available will cause irreparable damage, with the underprivileged disproportionately harmed' *(all counter to lower right).*

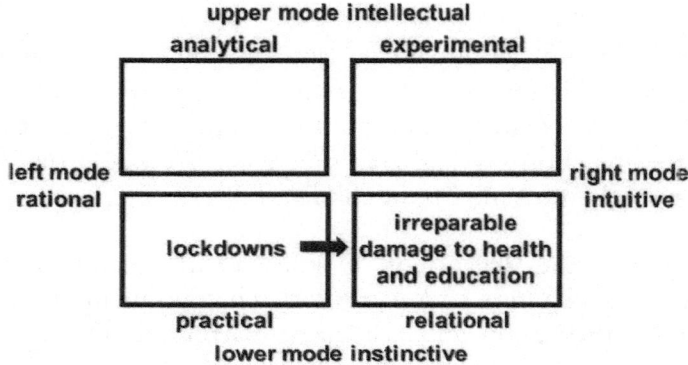

Devastating effects of lockdowns

'We know that all populations will eventually reach herd immunity – the point at which the rate of new infections is stable – and that this can be assisted by (but is not dependent upon) a vaccine. The most compassionate approach *(strong lower right)* that balances the risks and benefits of reaching herd immunity, is to allow those who are at minimal risk of death to live their lives normally to build up immunity to the virus through natural infection, while better protecting those who are at highest risk.'

Some commentators interpreted 'build up immunity to the virus through natural infection' as 'letting the virus rip'. Challenged to come up with a middle way, between lockdowns and 'letting the virus rip', in November 2020 the authors described in more detail the concept of Focused Protection.

They recognised that public health is concerned with the health and well-being *(strong lower right)* of populations in a broader way than just infection control.

The aim of Focused Protection is to minimize overall mortality from both COVID-19 and other diseases by balancing the need to protect high-risk individuals from COVID-19 while reducing the harm that lockdowns have had on other aspects of medical care and public health.

The Declaration outlined two facts: 'Firstly, anyone can get infected. Children have lower mortality from COVID-19 than from the annual influenza. For people under the age of 70, the infection survival rate is 99.95%. We know that age is the single most important risk factor.

'Secondly, the harms of lockdown are manifold and devastating *(counter to lower right)*. The two main planks of Focused Protection and the Great Barrington Declaration follow logically *(strong upper left)* from these two facts.

'For older people and other high-risk groups, COVID-19 is a deadly disease that should be met with overwhelming resources aimed at protecting them wherever they are, whether in nursing homes, at their own home, in the workplace, or in multi-generational homes.'

(By including the workplace, the authors emphasise that protection needs to be focussed on those needing it. Workplaces can remain open whilst protecting the very few workers who are vulnerable.)

'For the non-vulnerable, who face far greater harm from lockdowns than they do from COVID-19 infection risk, the lockdowns should be lifted *(avoid lower left)* and – for those who so decide – normal life resumed.' The non-vulnerable would follow good public health practice and wear masks, socially distance, wash hands often, stay at home when sick, and so on.

The authors concluded: 'Inconsistent with the standard pandemic preparedness plans that existed before the COVID-19 epidemic, lockdowns are, and have always been, a radical approach to infection control. Focused Protection is the middle ground that will end the pandemic with the least harm to the vulnerable and non-vulnerable alike.'

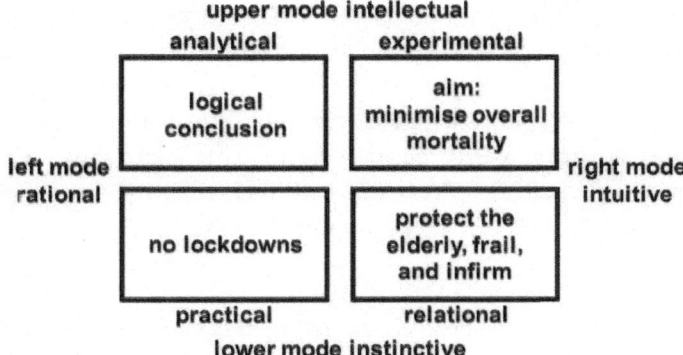

The cognitive diversity of Focused Protection in the Great Barrington Declaration

'Lockdown policies should be rejected'

In January 2022 three economists at Johns Hopkins University in the US - Jonas Herby, Prof Lars Jonung, and Prof Steve H. Hanke – released a report (27) arguing that lockdown policies should be rejected. It was an examination of data from a number of independent studies of the same subject, in order to determine overall trends in the US. It was later published as a book *Did Lockdowns Work?* by the Institute for Economic Affairs.

The review used an 'empirical approach' - meaning it used real-world data and not modelling or estimates. It argued that COVID-19 deaths were reduced as follows: 2.9% by stay-at-home orders, 4.4% by school closures, 10.6% by business closures, and 0.1% by border closures, but only 0.2% overall by lockdowns.

The review concluded that the benefits of lockdowns were 'marginal at best' and needed to be compared with their 'devastating effects' on health, education, society, and the economy. They concluded that: 'Lockdown policies are ill-founded and should be rejected as a pandemic policy instrument.'

Baroness Hallett, chair of the COVID-19 Inquiry, has been accused of 'stonewalling' and 'censorship' after refusing the review research as official evidence. Bhattacharya and Hanke have also documented that covid-related research papers by various authors were censored on the platforms *Social Science Research Network* (SSRN) and *medRxiv*. Censorship reflects very strong controlling *lower left* thinking.

Facebook founder Mark Zuckerberg has said Facebook and Instagram were wrong to censor posts about COVID-19 during the pandemic.

In a letter to a US Congress committee Zuckerberg wrote: 'In 2021, senior officials from the Biden administration, including the White House, repeatedly pressured our teams for months to censor certain COVID-19 content... and expressed a lot of frustration with our teams when we didn't agree... I also think we made some choices that, with the benefit of hindsight and new information, we wouldn't make today.'

Charles Moore, the journalist and a former editor of *The Daily Telegraph, The Spectator,* and *The Sunday Telegraph*, has commented that the original, probably justifiable, emergency lockdown was over-extended, producing psychological and economic disaster.

'Groupthink silenced opponents of lockdowns'

Sarah Knapton, the Science Editor for *The Telegraph* wrote: 'Scientific groupthink *(strong upper left)* silenced those who disagreed with COVID lockdowns. Many influential scientists were ignored, ridiculed, and shunned for suggesting less draconian ways of dealing with the virus. For example, the signatories of the Great Barrington Declaration were pilloried and made to seem as if they were in the minority. A recent study by Stanford University revealed they were not; they just had fewer social media followers and so struggled in the face of more organised opposition.'

The author of the Stanford study, Prof John Ioannidis, said: "Twitter should not be used for arbitrating what is scientifically correct, let alone for shaping health policy. It can be easily usurped by agendas and narratives; it is very easily susceptible to political colouration and fads, and it is often used for smearing opponents. I worry about the distortion that can ensue when science is communicated in brief clips or with a mindset of how to satisfy or excite one's followers."

Knapton continued: 'Much of the pro-lockdown narrative was controlled by Independent Sage, a small group of scientists who effectively organised themselves *(strong lower left)* into a political movement which sought to influence policy. Even moderate scientists who called for greater evidence on lockdowns, masks, and other restrictions, faced the full force of supporters of the highly organised group. Many academics and researchers were scared of losing grant funding if they raised their heads above the parapet.'

Hence, a vociferous minority on social media made it appear that most scientists believed in greater restrictions.

Knapton continued: 'Even within the Government, there is now a feeling that too much attention was paid to too narrow a band of scientists at the expense of seeing the bigger picture *(avoiding upper right).'*

A government minister said: "Public health officials who have absolutely no remit to keep the economy vibrant, whose only remit is to make sure there is no infection, were calling for everything to be shut down *(very strong lower left control)."*

Knapton felt that early guidance by Ofcom actually encouraged groupthink. Ofcom warned broadcasters against programmes or news reports featuring advice which discouraged the audience from following official rules.

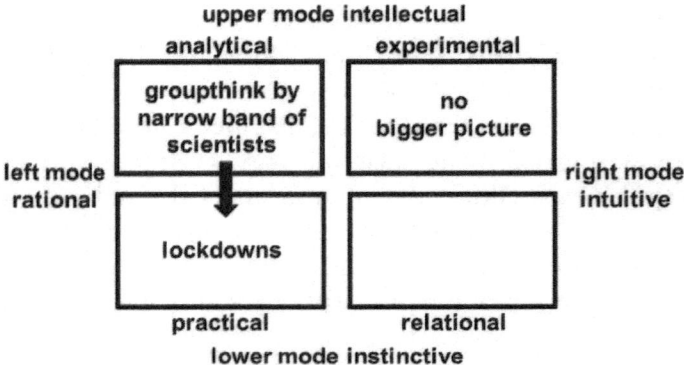

'Groupthink avoided the bigger picture'

Canadian economist Professor Alex Tabarrok said: "So-called science advisers often represented one discipline when what was required was integrating insights *(upper right)* from many disciplines *(all four quadrants)* with careful consideration of trade-offs and uncertainty *(lower left)*." Prof Tabarrok clearly recommends a cognitive diversity approach in all four quadrants of thinking:

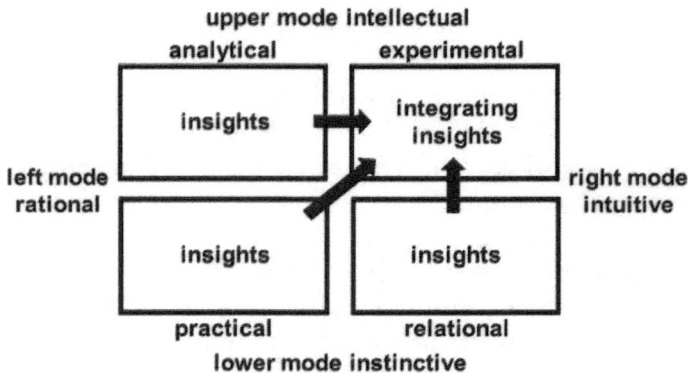

'What was required was integrating insights'

152

Social media companies helped anti-vaxxers

A consultant in charge of an intensive care unit stated that the misinformation put forward by the COVID-deniers, the conspiracy theorists, the anti-vaxxers and others - mainly via social media - was having a catastrophic effect by '...undermining the monumental efforts of the NHS.'

The Centre for Countering Digital Hate reported how social media companies cynically helped anti-vaxx networks gain 58 million followers, generating up to $1bn a year in advertising and other revenues, threatening the effectiveness of vaccine campaigns.

An outcome was that by August 2021 some 90% of patients on ventilators were anti-vaxxers. Instead of scarce hospital resources being redirected into addressing the backlog caused by COVID-19, it was reported that they were being consumed by totally unnecessary new cases of COVID-19.

It is on record that many anti-vaxxers went to their deaths regretting not being vaccinated.

The first signs of proof that mass vaccination is the most powerful tool against COVID-19 emerged in Israel. In early February 2021, analysis by the Weizmann Institute of Science at Tel Aviv University showed that cases and hospital admissions in Israel were falling steeply among vaccinated age groups.

In January 2021, before vaccination was introduced in the UK, some 60,000 cases per day were leading to 1,300 deaths per day (2.2% of cases). Once vaccination was introduced, the numbers of infections and deaths plummeted.

By May 2021 as vaccination rollout accelerated, some 2,800 cases per day were leading to only 4 deaths per day (0.2% of cases).

'UK should make better use of data'

The Data Evaluation and Learning for Viral Epidemics (DELVE) Group of the Royal Society has said the Government should make better use of data gathered by private companies, rather than by sticking with its centralised data gathering approach. By not adding private sector data to state data, the UK was not being innovative *(avoiding upper right thinking)*.

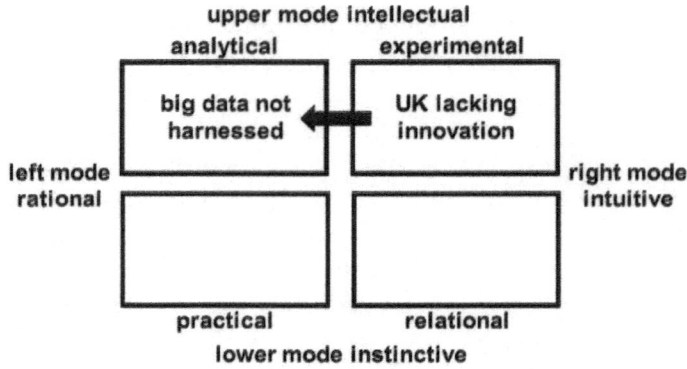

'UK lacking in innovation'

In Spain, the counts of the daily flow of people from one place to another between more than 3,000 districts were available to the authorities at the click of a button. This was based on a collaboration between the country's three main mobile phone operators.

DELVE claimed that this approach allowed Spanish officials to have a deeper understanding of how the movement of people contributed to the spread of the virus. Spain was one of the few European nations which avoided a second national lockdown, though transmission of the disease was still high, resulting in local lockdowns.

Neil Lawrence, professor of machine learning at the University of Cambridge said: "The UK has talked about making better use of data for the public good, but we have had statements of good intent, rather than action... there is a wealth of other data, such as from transport systems. The more we understand about this pandemic, the better we can tackle it."

Prof Lawrence added: "We should be able to work together *(lower left)*, the private and the public sectors, to harness big data *(upper left)* for massive positive social good *(upper right strategic aim)* and do that safely *(lower left)* and responsibly *(lower right)*." In this one sentence, Prof Lawrence employed all of cognitive diversity.

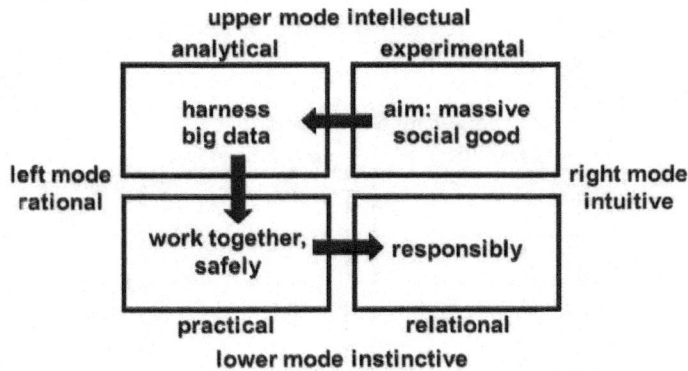

Prof Lawrence's cognitive diversity approach

The Delta wave of mid 2021

The Delta variant of COVID-19 hit the UK in mid–May 2021. With the easing of lockdown 3 by late July 2021, SAGE experts had predicted Britain could face more than 100,000 cases a day by August. Yet in July 2021 the actual number peaked at 49,000 leading to 60 deaths per day (0.1% of cases) and was falling.

The Office for National Statistics estimated that nine out of ten adults were now immune to COVID-19. Perhaps a return to normal working was now possible? Not quite...

In the third week of July 2021 over 600,000 people were 'pinged' by the COVID-19 app to self-isolate. In addition, 934,000 children were sent home from school. However, out of almost 2.3 million people told to self-isolate, only 11.4% actually tested positive, and the hospitalisation rate was of the order of 0.1% of cases.

Nevertheless, 'pingdemic' replaced pandemic, and shutdown *(strong lower left control)* replaced lockdown as workers in retail, transport, tourism, manufacturing, the NHS, and police were told to self-isolate. Supermarket shelves that were full during lockdown were now empty during shutdown - shades of post-war rationing which lasted longer than the Second World War!

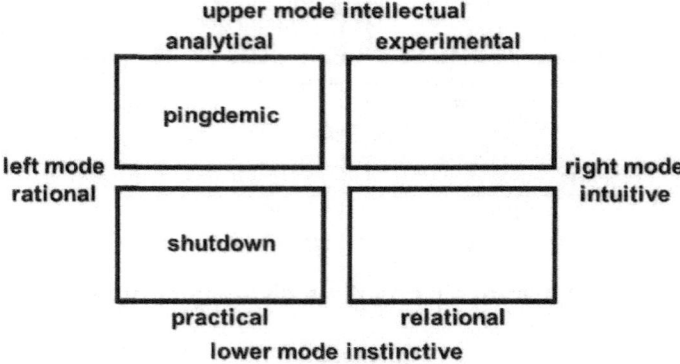

Pingdemic replaced pandemic, shutdown replaced lockdown

The self-isolation rules that sparked the 'pingdemic' were finally relaxed on 16 August 2021 due to the success of the vaccine rollout. Those who had been double vaccinated, or under 18 years of age, were no longer required to isolate for ten days if 'pinged'.

Britain's world-beating vaccination programme had broken the chain between infections and rates of serious illness and death. Figures would eventually show that the unvaccinated are up to 32 times more likely than the double-vaccinated to die if they catch COVID-19.

The Omicron wave of late 2021

The Omicron variant hit the UK on 27 November 2021. In mid-December 2021, SAGE urged the government to introduce "more stringent measures" *(strong lower left lockdown)* to cope with the Omicron wave, after models warned hospitalisations could peak at between 3,000 and 10,000 a day and deaths at between 600 and 6,000 a day.

It is understood that UK ministers were by now concerned that SAGE did not fully consider the damage to the economy, mental health, and education from lockdown. Therefore, after taking advice from outside SAGE, the Government chose not to bring in restrictions, and deaths peaked at 306 on 21 January 2022 while daily hospital admissions never rose beyond some 2,600.

The correlation between death and infections was very low: some 0.1%. Whilst Omicron was very infectious, the combination of vaccinations, herd immunity and a mutated, milder virus all resulted in a very low death rate.

Prof Graham Medley, the chairman of the Scientific Pandemic Influenza Group on Modelling (Spi-M), warned that modelling could not "accurately predict the numbers" and said predicting which of the scenarios would happen was just 'guesswork'. Dr Tom Jefferson, of the University of Oxford said: "...(SAGE) should have gone a long time ago. The modellers have a track record of getting things wrong."

The BMJ recommendations

By way of providing context and taking an *upper right* big picture view of different strategies, it is useful here to mention what other countries did. The *British Medical Journal* identified three strategies used by Governments around the world for dealing with COVID-19 (28).

The very detailed report is well worth reading and is very briefly summarised below.

Aggressive containment

Asian and Pacific countries such as China, New Zealand and Singapore aimed to eliminate community transmission and achieve elimination status (zero-COVID) for 28 consecutive days. Initial lockdowns were more stringent and longer *(very strong lower left)* than in countries pursuing other strategies. These Asian countries viewed the route to economic recovery as only possible by containing the pandemic.

Learning from past experiences with the SARS outbreak in 2003, China and Singapore had strengthened their preparedness for public health emergencies *(strong upper right strategic planning)*. China's strict zero-COVID strategy aimed to stamp out all outbreaks and chains of transmission using border controls, mass testing, quarantines, and stringent lockdowns; this led to serious public dissent and riots.

In May 2022, the World Health Organisation (WHO) reported that China had less than zero excess deaths per 100,000 across 2020-2021. However, the head of the WHO Dr Tedros Adhanom Ghebreyesus warned that China's stringent zero-COVID strategy was "not sustainable" in the face of the highly contagious Omicron variant.

China's resources focused on relentless testing, contact tracing and quarantining at the expense of an effective vaccination strategy.

Suppression

Countries such as the US and Argentina aimed to suppress and minimise community infections. Countries that aimed for suppression saw a trade-off between public health measures and economic growth, emphasising economic recovery during relaxation periods.

Partisan politics in the US led to mixed messages and lack of commitment from the government to mount a timely and effective response to the pandemic, resulting in large loss of life, including a family friend. US political leaders discredited scientific advisers, contributing to delay and lack of coordination in its COVID-19 response.

The US and Argentina were less prepared than Uganda, partially owing to limited experiences of responding to large scale epidemics or underfunded public health systems.

Mitigation

Countries aimed to protect the health systems by flattening the epidemic curve (UK) or achieving herd immunity in the population (Sweden). The public health interventions focused on protecting vulnerable and high-risk groups while allowing transmission among low-risk groups.

The UK initially aimed for mitigation but shifted towards suppression, marked by the announcement of lockdown 1 in March 2020. Sweden, which was criticised in the early stages of the pandemic for resisting a mandatory lockdown, had fewer deaths per capita than much of Europe.

In May 2022, the WHO reported that Sweden had 56 excess deaths per 100,000 across 2020-2021 – compared to 109 in the UK, 111 in Spain, 116 in Germany and 133 in Italy.

Public health interventions

Each strategy used different combinations of public health interventions. Population based interventions included lockdowns, face masks, social distancing, and personal hygiene. Case based interventions included case detection, contact tracing of confirmed cases, isolation, and surveillance of cases. Border control measures included travel restrictions for travellers from high-risk countries or mandatory quarantine requirements.

Key messages of the report

The report can be summarised in the BMJ diagram:

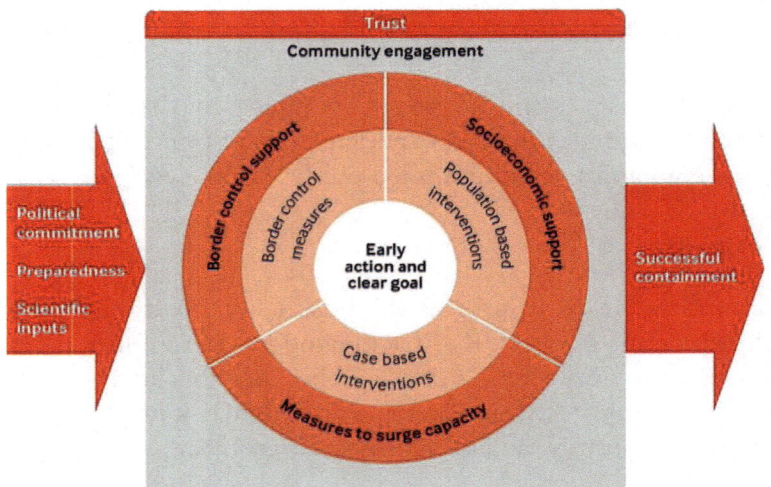

Credit: BMJ

Vaccines were not available until 2021. In the absence of vaccines and treatments, aggressive containment of community transmission is the optimal strategy in emerging pandemics to save lives and protect the economy.

Aggressive containment might not be sustainable in the long term. A more sustainable approach, which amalgamates acceptable levels of community transmission and high vaccination rates, may be the best way forward.

Successful containment requires countries to take immediate action in response to emerging outbreaks and clearly define the targets for relaxing interventions.

A comprehensive package of public health interventions needs to be implemented stringently with support measures for mitigating the adverse effects and increasing capacity.

Success is underpinned by trust and community engagement, facilitated by strong political commitment, well prepared public health systems, and scientific input into policy making.

The key messages of the *BMJ* diagram can also be presented by using a Cognitive Diversity At Work™ view:

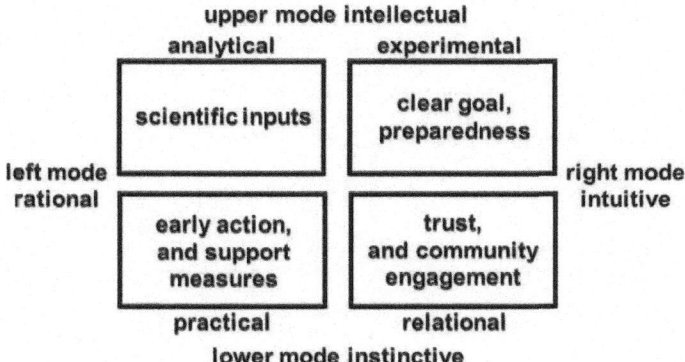

**The key messages of the BMJ report:
a Cognitive Diversity At Work™ view**

SAGE stands down

By March 2022 SAGE had stood down, and all legal restrictions in England were lifted under the 'Living With COVID' plan.

Professor Carl Heneghan, the director of the Centre for Evidence-Based Medicine at the University of Oxford, said: "This is a remarkable turnabout of events given that just before Christmas 2021, SAGE advisers were warning infections could hit two million per day and were pushing for further restrictions.

"The Government will need to review whether SAGE is fit for purpose when it comes to pandemics, particularly given its lack of clinical input and its overreliance on modelling – which we now know is no more than 'guesswork' – and its tendency to fixate on a particular set of assumptions."

The UK's COVID-19 cognitive diversity profile

In summing up this chapter, I show below an indicative cognitive diversity profile of the UK Government's handling of the pandemic:

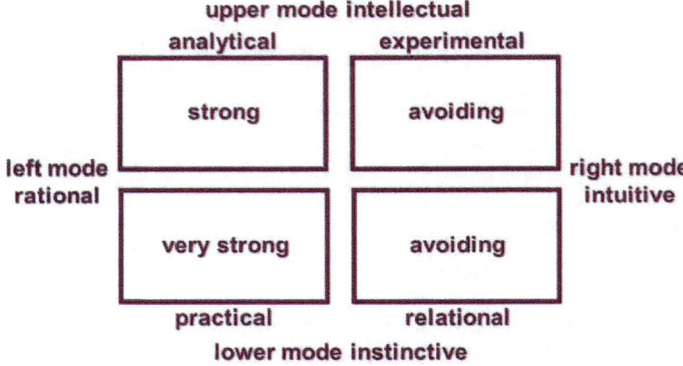

Indicative cognitive diversity profile of the UK Government's handling of COVID-19

Upper left analytical thinking

Overall, a strong preference. The UK had strong scientific thinking, with the Executive following the advice of SAGE, albeit with the risk of groupthink. Independent specialists have commented that the advice was over-reliant on error-prone mathematical modelling.

Lockdown laws were introduced under secondary legislation, which allowed ministers to create emergency legislation without prior parliamentary approval or meaningful parliamentary debate, contrary to custom and practice.

Lower left practical thinking

Overall, a very strong preference. The UK went to the nth degree in devising lockdowns and ever more complicated safety measures requiring compulsion without differentiation.

A survey found nine out of 10 police officers thought the measures were unclear. It was reported that even the top police officer responsible for their enforcement did not fully understand them. The myriad of rules and regulations left most people confused.

Lower right relational thinking

Overall, an avoiding preference. SAGE, COBRA, and the Executive avoided giving due weight to *lower right relational thinking*. Independent specialists claim that the UK safety measures inflicted devastating effects on short and long-term public health both physical and mental, greater excess mortality in years to come, burdening the poor and the young, impacting education, and inculcating fear.

Upper right experimental/strategic thinking

Overall, an avoiding preference. SAGE, COBRA, and the Executive avoided giving due weight to *upper right* experimental/strategic thinking resulting in lack of vision, innovation, imagination, and a holistic view.

Overall, UK Government thinking has been very strongly in the *rational left mode*. In layman's terms one might say a left brained, half-brained approach.

Recommendations

Cognitive Diversity At Work™ makes the following recommendations for dealing with a new coronavirus pandemic.

A strategic planning team

The UK Government assembles a strategic planning team including relevant economic, educational, health and social care professionals. The team must reflect strong thinking in all four quadrants: analytical, practical, relational, and experimental. This would introduce strong *intuitive right mode* thinking to balance the current *rational left mode* bias.

It is not sufficient to expect existing left mode thinkers on committees to try to think situationally in intuitive right mode ways, or vice versa. It is not sufficient to expect existing intellectual mode thinkers on committees to try to think situationally in instinctive mode ways, or vice versa.

A strategic plan

The strategic planning team learns the lessons from COVID-19 and produces an agreed strategic plan for coping with a future coronavirus pandemic, the plan to be reviewed periodically, and available off-the-shelf when necessary.

Learn from best practice

Learn from best practice in other countries; Bill Gates, billionaire founder of Microsoft, posted in a blog, 'Ever since I was a teenager, I've tackled every big new problem the same way: by starting off with two questions...who has dealt with this problem well, and what can we learn from them?'

Formulate the right aims

The strategic plan must be careful when stating its aims. For example, the message to the people at the start of COVID-19 lockdown was: "You must stay at home. The single most important action we can all take is to stay at home to protect the NHS and save lives." If the message had been "The single most important action we can all take is to protect the vulnerable", then the actions taken would have been very different. The strategic plan must reflect the aim of public health interventions, which is the least overall impact to society as a whole. This includes a plan for avoiding hospital-acquired infection from day one.

Prevent groupthink

SAGE and or COBRA to be reconstituted to include strong right mode thinking to challenge the very strong left mode thinking that prevailed during COVID-19. SAGE to include voices of dissenting science to prevent groupthink.

Counter negative propaganda

Find communication specialists to counter any negative propaganda spread on social media by groups such as COVID-deniers, conspiracy theorists, and anti-vaxxers. Find technical specialists to prevent such propaganda. He who shouts loudest is not necessarily in the right.

Find the real problem

When problem-solving, find the real problem. Stating the real problem often suggests the right solution.

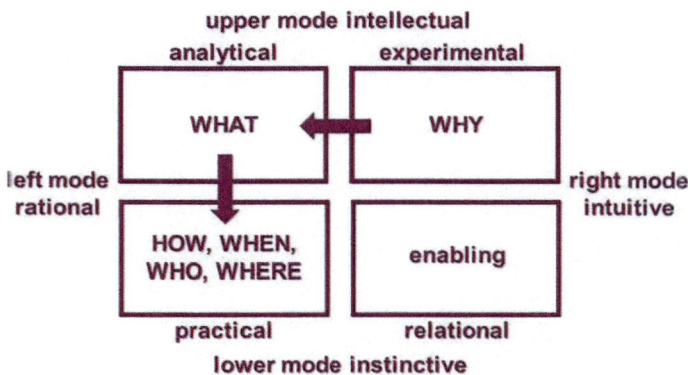

"Why?" is the first and most important question of all.

Conclusion and Next Steps

In this book you have learned what cognitive diversity is, and how it reveals precious insights into what is really going on around you at work. How it is above identity diversity, and how it is fully inclusive of others' thinking.

How it reveals why you have misunderstandings, mistakes, false understandings, confrontation, tribal groupthink, or even synergy with other people at work. Why you work well with some people and not with others.

How it reveals insights into stereotyping, job satisfaction, emotional intelligence, women in STEM, entrepreneurship, bureaucracy, challenges facing lawyers, doctors, and teachers at work, and the UK's handling of COVID-19.

How you can get higher performance through improving your communicating, collaborating, decision-making, problem-solving, coaching, mentoring, counselling and customer relations.

How you can get higher productivity and staff retention, more creativity and innovation, and quicker job-mastery.

To unlock these benefits, your first step is to obtain your cognitive diversity Individual Profile. This paves the way for Pair Profiling, Team Profiling, Organisation Profiling, and training in communications, problem-solving, and decision-making. Just go to www.cognitivediversity.co.uk/profiling.

Thinking is free and brain-based. As a bonus, I strongly recommend you undertake training in Neuro-Linguistic Programming, which addresses the whole of the nervous system, and perfectly complements cognitive diversity.

Acknowledgements

I deeply appreciate the kindness of Sally Bishop who certified me as a Herrmann HBDI® Certified Practitioner in Whole Brain® Thinking in 2004. Sally Bishop was trained by Ned Herrmann and introduced Whole Brain® Thinking to the UK.

I am very glad for the on-going Learning and Development opportunities with the thought leaders at the Herrmann® organisation. I especially appreciate the kindness of Victoria Lincoln who greatly helped with my understanding of the Herrmann® organisation, and Anne Griswold who upgraded my certification in 2017.

Regarding this book, I deeply appreciate the kindness of the following: Kate Graham for proof reading, Steve Woodard for improving its look and appeal technically, and Ray Tooley for being such a supportive sounding board during our many walks over the South Downs.

References

1. The Association for Project Management Body of Knowledge 7th Edition.

2. *The Whole Brain Business Book Second Edition*, ©1996-2015 by Ned Herrmann and Ann Herrmann-Nehdi, McGraw-Hill. Copyright material is used with permission.

3. *Diversity Best Practices*, Abbott Laboratories, © 2009, New York.

4. *Extraordinary Minds: Portraits Of 4 Exceptional Individuals And An Examination Of Our Own Extraordinariness*, Howard E. Gardner, copyright © 1997. Reprinted by permission of Basic Books, an imprint of Hachette Book Group, Inc.

5. The four-colour, four-quadrant graphic, and Whole Brain® are registered trademarks of Herrmann Global LLC. Copyright material is used with permission.

6. *First World War*, Martin Gilbert, copyright ©1994, Weidenfeld and Nicolson.

7. ONS: Table 1 *The top 20 expected jobs versus reality, UK, 2011-2012, 2017.*

8. UK Social Mobility Commission Sixth Report, *Social mobility in Great Britain – state of the nation 2018 to 2019.*

9. 30percentclub.org.

10. *Female entrepreneurs and the curse of 'male-only' business attributes,* The Conversation, © 2017.

11. *A Comparison of Four Scales Predicting Entrepreneurship,* J.C. Huefner, H.K. Hunt, and Robinson P.N., Academy of Entrepreneurship Journal, Volume 1, Number 2, Fall 1996.

12. www.sands.org.uk/sands-united.

13. *My Sister Milly,* Gemma Dowler, copyright © 2017, Penguin Random House.

14. *British Medical Journal* 2018;363:k4530 © 2021.

15. *House of Commons Library Briefing Paper CBP 7222* dated 16 December 2019, licensed under the Open Parliament Licence v3.0.

16. Ofqual: alytics.ofqual.gov.uk/apps/Alevel/Outcomes/

17. DfE: explore-education-statistics.service.gov.uk/find-statistics/a-level-and-other-16-to-18-results.

18. Office for National Statistics Nomis *Annual Population Survey - Employment by Occupation (SOC2020) by Sex for 2022.*

19. *STEM Learning* stem.org.uk

20. https://www.worldlifeexpectancy.com/selected-deaths-vs-covid-19-united-kingdom.

21. *The Year The World Went Mad: a Scientific Memoir,* Prof Mark Woolhouse, copyright ©2022, Sandstone Press Ltd.

22. Office for National Statistics data *(Table 6a, referencetables, www.ons.gov.uk)*

23. *Forgotten Voices of the Blitz and the Battle For Britain,* copyright © Joshua Levine and The Imperial

War Museum 2006, Ebury Press, reproduced by permission of The Random House Group Ltd.

24.   *Breathtaking: Inside the NHS in a Time of Pandemic,* Dr Rachel Clarke MD, copyright ©2021, Little, Brown and Company.

25.   *Intensive Care: a GP, a Community & COVID-19,* Dr Gavin Francis GP, copyright ©2021, Wellcome Collection.

26.   https://gbdeclaration.org/

27.   *A Literature Review And Meta-Analysis Of The Effects Of Lockdowns On Covid-19 Mortality* , Jonas Herby, Lars Jonung, and Steve H. Hanke, 2022, Studies in Applied Economics.

28.   *BMJ 2021;375:e067508,* British Medical Journal, 2021, distributed under the terms of the Creative Commons Attribution IGO License.

About the Author

Photo by Mark Kemp

Michael Davis BSc(Eng), MBA

Michael Davis is Director of Cognitive Diversity Ltd, a Certified Practitioner in Whole Brain® Thinking, Master Practitioner in NLP, performance coach, mentor and trainer.

As an engineer, executive, interim executive, and consultant he has worked with people who think differently, in different cultures, in all phases of technical projects and business change, in the public and private sectors, in academia, and in small, medium and large organisations, both nationally and internationally.

Herrmann
Certified
Practitioner

cognitivediversity.co.uk
mdpml.co.uk
projectmanagercoaching.com